D0221562

BLACK'S

DICTIONARY OF
PHYSICAL
EDUCATION
AND SCHOOL SPORT

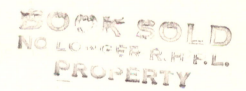

BLACK'S
DICTIONARY OF
PHYSICAL
EDUCATION
AND SCHOOL SPORT

Gareth Williams, Sarah Pinder,
Alan Thomson and
Dean Williams

Note
Whilst every effort has been made to ensure that the content of this book is as technically accurate and as sound as possible, neither the author nor the publishers can accept responsibility for any injury or loss sustained as a result of the use of this material.

Published by A&C Black Publishers Ltd
36 Soho Square, London W1D 3QY
www.acblack.com

ISBN 978 1 4081 2368 3

A CIP catalogue record for this book is available from the British Library.

Acknowledgements
Cover photograph © Shutterstock
Illustrations by Jeff Edwards
Designed by James Watson
Commissioned by Charlotte Croft
Edited by David Pearson

This book is produced using paper that is made from wood grown in managed, sustainable forests. It is natural, renewable and recyclable. The logging and manufacturing processes conform to the environmental regulations of the country of origin.

Typeset in 11pt on 14pt Haarlemmer MT by Palimpsest Book Production Limited, Falkirk, Stirlingshire

Printed and bound in Great Britain by Martins the Printers

Contents

Acknowledgements and Foreword   vii

Introduction   1

Dictionary   5

List of Abbreviations   199

Bibliography   203

Dedicated to all those pupils and colleagues who have made the teaching of physical education and school sport such a fulfilling and rewarding experience.

ACKNOWLEDGEMENTS

The authors would like to thank colleagues at Edge Hill University for time spent reading through draft material and for providing invaluable advice. Your support and expertise is much appreciated.

FOREWORD

This book will provide an invaluable resource for students at all levels who need to make sense of baseline concepts in the world of physical education and school sport.

In providing definitions and illustrative examples of a wide range of professional and academic concepts, terms, names and titles it will prove a valuable reference for a breadth of vocational and academic assignments and tasks. The authors are to be congratulated on providing a comprehensive and accessible text that fills a niche in the study of physical education and school sport.

Professor Ken Green: Editor, European Physical Education Review; Professor and Head, Department of Sport & Exercise Sciences, University of Chester; Visiting Professor of Physical Education at the Norwegian School Of Sports Sciences.

INTRODUCTION

Sport has had and will continue to have a considerable impact on life in the 21st century. Media coverage appears to become increasingly intense while at the same time the public are urged to get physically active as considerable amounts of public and private money are being invested in facilities. In education schools find that sport is a popular examination option and at higher education level degree-related courses continue to flourish. But what has happened to physical education (PE)? Why have recent government initiatives in schools promoted 'sport' in their titles, often at the expense of 'PE'? These are issues that perhaps reflect the standing of a subject that has been contested like no other on the school curriculum. Furthermore, understanding battles over terminology, curriculum, pedagogy and gender will help us to understand why PE is where it is today.

However, the reality is that as this introduction is being written there is a general consensus that 'physical education and school sport' (PESS) has been accepted as the appropriate term for what is happening in schools. Hence the purpose of this book: to inform the reader as to what is currently going on and to disentangle some of the threads that have led to this current situation with the hope of stimulating further discussion. This will prove to be a helpful guide for undergraduates to help them meet the demands of a PESS-related higher education course. It will also be useful for new teachers of PESS in providing both background information and teaching tips to help them as they embark on their career. The book then will ultimately reflect the current PESS situation in schools; each entry is written so that the reader can apply the content to a number of different settings primarily based on the education of 4–18-year-old children in the United Kingdom.

PE has changed immeasurably from its beginnings, which were characterised by a social class divide between the games-playing private schools in the latter part of the 19th century and the forms of drill imposed upon the state elementary schools in the early part of the 20th century. Between the wars a focus on health began to dominate within state schools and PE became the domain of middle-class female teachers also keen to promote dance and gymnastics. After World War Two returning service men entered the profession bringing with them their ideas on games and fitness. It was also this period in time which saw many state schools attempt to copy a dominant games-playing model used by the privately run public schools. PE then became an area of conflict between those female teachers who wanted to retain an emphasis on free expression and creativity and those males who aimed to promote PE as sport.

It is in the last twenty years, though, that education has undergone its most dramatic transformation. This is the culmination of a culture change initiated in the late 1980s which has subjected large sections of the public sector to market forces. As a result schools have become very competitive institutions often run, at times, as increasingly isolated business units. PE itself has become embroiled in the need to achieve with the resultant growth in examination courses and a plethora of initiatives often underpinned by a desire for political gain. Much of this recent activity is a result of the fact that PE has traditionally had to fight for its status on the school curriculum. As a predominantly physical activity involving the use of gross musculature there have been many qualms concerning its validity and at times it has appeared that the PE profession have almost tried to 'reinvent' the subject to enhance its credibility.

However, there is a strong feeling that at the time of writing PE is in the ascendant and it is the aim of this book to provide an update on the more recent issues such as the drive to improve the nation's health, the desire to regenerate communities and the quest for discovering young sporting talent. As Britain moves towards the 2012 Olympics we can perhaps expect more of the same with continuing government initiatives ultimately trying to justify significant public expenditure on sport. This book would hope to be a beacon for 2012, a source of information for the build-up and a legacy for the aftermath.

Selected entries reflect the notion that PE is an eclectic amalgam of topics, a multidisciplinary concept that suggests a unique level of understanding. Few other subjects demand such comprehension. Hence socio-cultural entries within this book borrow from the study of history and sociology. Pedagogical aspects reflect philosophical and psychological concerns while scientific entries borrow from biology, anatomy and physiology. Even then, sub-divisions may be made with specific areas of study influenced by political sociology and child development. A unique feature of the book is that it includes sections devoted to career guidance for aspiring teachers with invaluable advice concerning both safeguarding children and health and safety concerns. Other entries provide help for students about to engage with research methods, again with specific relevance to PESS.

This book will primarily be of use to those who are starting a course at university for the first time and who may well be unaware of the relationship between PE and sport. For practical assessments new PE students often engage in 'coaching' rather than 'teaching', failing to fully understand the difference between the two. Such individuals are sometimes driven by an initial career desire to establish winning teams within a school setting. Trying to explain how sport is used as a medium through PE can take time and recent government statements that place the two terms together can only add to the confusion. The sooner undergraduate students are made aware of this the better and this book will aid readers in that process. Consequently, certain sections are written to reflect this tension between sport and PE, an uneasy relationship which is both historical and contemporary. It is perhaps this one topic which overrides initial perceptions of the subject, often leading to misconceptions and misunderstanding.

The entries selected reflect modules currently taught as part of an undergraduate degree in PESS. There are many more that could have been included and the authors would welcome discussion on any such omissions. Nevertheless, selected content has been the result of much discussion and the book should be seen as a reflection of the state of PESS at the time of writing. No doubt there will be many more new initiatives to come, particularly as PESS moves to support the 2012 Olympics and future revised updated editions of this text may be required. The writers have used both quantitative and qualitative research, much of it from a secondary source. Socio-cultural aspects have been written predominantly using critical theory, although other theoretical standpoints have been used as well in some entries. The guidance on further reading can be used to stimulate extra discussion.

This dictionary should be used as an initial reference point for students of PESS. It is this starting point that is so important for those who are faced with both new concepts and terminology that requires a quick, precise interpretation in order to facilitate understanding. All entries are cross-referenced to help you find your way to related subjects. This dictionary should be returned to as a revision guide – the concise entries are a useful recapping of core information. Some of the content will cover new topics reflecting the very latest government initiatives in PESS. These are the sections that will aid both new and prospective PE teachers by providing up-to-date information along with some comment on how such topics link together both in a historical and in a contemporary sense.

The authors are excited by the opportunities that this book will provide for the PE profession. We are all former practitioners of the subject in schools and some of us have had responsibility for its management and development. As the study of sport has become increasingly academic in recent years we are determined that this subject, which has been the source of joy and achievement for so many people, should not miss out on such scrutiny and appraisal. We hope that the book will stimulate and inspire, challenge and guide, so that PE in whatever form it takes will continue to flourish towards and beyond 2012.

ACCIDENTS IN PESS

The *Oxford English Dictionary* defines an 'accident' as 'an unfortunate incident that happens unexpectedly and unintentionally' or 'an incident that happens by chance or without apparent cause'. The Health and Safety Executive (HSE) expand on this in their definition: 'any unplanned event that results in injury or ill-health to people or damages property or materials, but where there was risk of harm.' Teachers of PE should plan activities with consideration to *risk management* along with the minimising of potential for injury and harm to pupils. However, due to the nature of the subject and despite rigorous risk assessment and management on behalf of the teacher, accidents will and do happen in PESS. Preventable accidents can occur where the teacher does not plan, prepare or take necessary precautions. Pupils are more prone to injuries in some activities than others.

Severs (2006), in an analysis of 330 PE-related accidents reported to the HSE in a two-year period, found that games provided a high proportion of the injuries, with tackling being the main cause. There were 62 accidents in gymnastics, 17 in trampolining and 14 in athletics. In order to minimise the potential for accidents and harm, teachers need to undertake thorough risk assessments and plan work that is progressive and at the right developmental level for the pupils in question. The teacher must also consider the selection of equipment and the organisation of the group and teaching environment. Where accidents do occur in PESS, the teacher(s) need to be conversant with the accident procedures in place within the school/local authority. Specific considerations need to be given in terms of whether the accident occurred in the gym, sports hall or swimming pool or out on the playing field, but general principles of management of the scene by the teacher can be employed. Katene and Edmonson (in Capel, ed., 2004) suggest that the teacher must remain calm and swiftly assess the situation, ensure that other pupils in the group are safe, attend to the needs of the injured pupil and call for assistance if required. Telephones should be easily accessible in the department, but where this is not possible, for example on the playing field, the teacher can carry a mobile phone to alert the school office or any other identified school contact. Otherwise, two pupils should be sent to summon help.

See also: *Accident Reporting and Recording, Risk Assessment/Management*

FURTHER READING

Association for Physical Education (AfPE), *Safe Practice in Physical Education and School Sport* (Coachwise, 2008)

Severs, J., 'Accidents in Physical Education, an Analysis of Injuries Reported to the Health and Safety Executive', *Physical Education Matters,* Summer (2006), pp. 19–21

Severs, J. with Whitlam, P. & Woodhouse, J., *Safety and Risk in Primary School Physical Education* (Routledge, 2003)

ACCIDENT REPORTING AND RECORDING

Once the initial accident has been dealt with appropriately and any injured parties assessed and treated as necessary, the process of recording and reporting the incident and subsequent actions must take place. All accidents need to be recorded in detail as soon as possible after the event. This is to ensure that necessary factual details are logged while they are still fresh in the minds of those involved. The details should be recorded on an Accident Report Form or in an Accident Book. The requirements and layout of these vary between local authorities and schools, but all should

a

contain some common essential details of the incident such as the name and age of the injured pupil, the date and the time the accident occurred, where it happened, the extent of the injuries sustained, any treatment given and subsequent actions taken. The form will also request the details of any witnesses to the accident and may provide a space for a supporting diagram to be drawn. The Association for Physical Education (AfPE) in their guidance *Safe Practice in Physical Education and School Sport* (AfPE, 2008), provide standardised and well-documented examples of forms and suggested accident procedures. AfPE emphasise that it is 'important that all accidents are recorded on the employers' official report form or accident book as soon as is reasonably possible. This aids the reporting process and is also useful in the event of a liability 'claim' (AfPE, 2008, p. 53).

Those accidents which have been documented must be reported in turn to the local authority or the HSE in order to comply with the 'Reporting of Injuries, Disease and Dangerous Occurrences Regulations' (RIDDOR, 1995). Reportable accidents include major injuries, defined as 'any resulting in death or injury requiring hospital treatment for any length of time, or injury that prevents the injured person attending work (or school) for more than three days' (AfPE, 2008, p. 53). This would also apply to some fractures, unconsciousness from electric shock or lack of oxygen and certain acute illnesses.

Good storage and record-keeping of accident reports is essential as the information they contain may need to be consulted for several years following the incident, for example if there is an ensuing legal case.

See also: *Accidents in PESS*

FURTHER READING

The Health and Safety Executive (HSE), *A Guide to the Reporting of Injuries, Disease and Dangerous Occurrences Regulations 1995* (HSE Books, 2008)

The Health and Safety Executive at www.hse.gov.uk

ACTIVEMARK

This award, along with Sportsmark and Sports Partnership Mark, is given to schools/partnerships for the delivery of high quality physical education and school sport (HQPESS) (*see separate entry*). Sports Partnership Mark provides recognition for School Sport Partnerships (SSPs) in their commitment to delivering HQPESS. Activemark is awarded to schools with primary-aged children and Sportsmark is awarded to schools that cater for secondary-aged children. All three of these kite marks are awarded to those schools/partnerships who have at least 90 per cent of pupils partaking in at least two hours of HQPESS a week.

Recognition for these awards is assessed via the National School Sports Survey, which collates registers taken by schools for pupil attendance at extra-curricular school sport activities. Another kite mark acknowledged by schools as a vital part of their community programme is Club Mark. This is awarded to external clubs who comply with minimum operating standards involving the appointment of personnel with the correct coaching qualifications. The same clubs are expected to also have effective policies in place for safeguarding children. In order for clubs to achieve accreditation for Club Mark award, they can receive advice from national governing bodies (NGBs) and/or County Sports Partnerships (CSPs) (*see separate entry*).

FURTHER READING

www.sportengland.org

www.teachernet.gov.uk

www.youthsporttrust.org

ADAPTATION (TO TRAINING)

The main objective of fitness training is to ensure changes occur in one or more of the body systems either through stress or overload, or by making them work harder than usual. The resulting long-term changes in the body are adaptations which in turn prove beneficial in enhancing or improving performance. Training must be continued in order to maintain these accrued benefits and if it is reduced or stopped, then the benefits will gradually be lost in accordance with the principle of reversibility.

The training intensity must be appropriately calculated if the desired training benefits are to be obtained. In terms of cardio-respiratory fitness, this may be achieved by training at a percentage of the VO2 max (maximal oxygen consumption), or at a percentage of the average maximum heart rate. Individuals can use age-predicted maximum heart rates to calculate a 'training sensitive zone' having a lower threshold of 70 per cent and an upper threshold of 90 per cent of the average maximum heart rate (McArdle et al., 2000). Work within this training zone over a period of time will promote aerobic adaptive responses.

Cardiovascular adaptations associated with endurance-based aerobic training include: cardiac hypertrophy (increase in size) with increases particularly in the left ventricle, increased stroke volume, reduced heart rate during sub-maximal exercise, increased cardiac output, increased blood volume and reduced blood pressure at rest.

There is still some debate surrounding the methods and benefits of living and training at altitude and subsequent performance at sea level (Wilmore & Costill, 2004). Nevertheless, altitude training is still utilised by endurance athletes in order to promote favourable physiological adaptations that aid performance in such events. These adaptations occur due to the reduced partial pressure of oxygen in the atmosphere and include corresponding increases in red blood cell count and the associated levels of haemoglobin. These are especially prominent when returning to compete at sea level.

Athletes in many activities rely on resistance training methods in order to stress the skeletal muscles and cause adaptations of benefit in exerting force or permitting muscles to work for prolonged periods. In order to make gains in strength, high intensity and low repetitions are required. Alternatively, low resistance and high repetitions will develop muscular endurance. The most notable adaptation to resistance training is an increase in the size of the muscle explained through muscle fibre 'hypertrophy', though McArdle et al. (2000, p. 412) suggest an increased fibre number (hyperplasia) provides for a suitable 'complementary hypothesis'; for example, where type II fibres reach maximum size. There is a corresponding strengthening of supporting connective tissues and bone with increases in muscle size and strength in order to protect muscles and joints from injury.

FURTHER READING

McArdle, W.D., Katch, F.I. & Katch, V. L., *Essentials of Exercise Physiology* (2nd edn, Lippincott Williams and Wilkins, 2000)

Wilmore, J.H., & Costill, D.L., *Physiology of Sport and Exercise* (Human Kinetics, 2004)

ANCIENT GREEKS

From approximately 1000 BC to 100 BC the Ancient Greeks progressed into a major European civilisation with the elevation of intellectual enquiry at the forefront of its development. Philosophy and religion were prominent throughout, although this was tempered by the need to protect and arm a nation often under threat from neighbours. Within Greece itself city states were at war with each other and so a culture of physicality emerged as young men prepared themselves for battle. This often manifested itself in public events of strength and endurance based on warrior sports. Competition took place at religious festivals alongside a ready association with Greek gods and mythological characters. When the athletes themselves began to assume professional status there was a sharp class divide between the aristocrats who could afford their own trainers and coaches and those from a poorer background who had to rely on city sponsorship and city-owned gymnasia. Sparta emerged as perhaps the most prominent of these states and here the preparation of athletes for festivals such as those at Olympia was taken very seriously.

The Greek philosophers themselves often poured scorn on athletes, denigrating the amount of time spent in training conducted at the expense of personal intellectual and spiritual development. Women were barred from taking part alongside men and also as spectators because this conflicted with Greek ideas about femininity. However, there was no doubting the mass appeal of these events and the legacy left from the festival at Olympia has contributed vastly to modern sport. Moreover, the city states of Sparta, Athena, Corinth and Helena have impacted upon 20th-century sporting language, particularly in English public schools. Kirk (2010) even suggests that Greek use of the term 'gymnastics' has historically helped the placement and positioning of this activity in 20th-century PE curriculums. Thus, advocates of gymnastics have not been afraid to call upon this aspect of its cultural heritage in the struggle to maintain its status. Munrow (1963) in particular heralded the Greeks' involvement with 'gymnastics' as a means of education through the body, using Plato's *The Republic* as his evidence.

Although the Romans (100 BC to AD 500) were keen to continue the Greek sporting festivals, many of them disintegrated, with the very last one held in AD 426. The new versions were more military based, with an even greater emphasis on preparing soldiers for battle. Soon sport became a means of social control, a way of appeasing the masses, with

a

chariot racing, boxing and athletics prominent. Roman emperors often used the games to court popularity, as epitomised by Nero's participation and subsequent attempts to cheat. The events became more barbaric, with activities such as bear- and bull-baiting prominent. The demise, caused by the Romans' increased influence in Greece, was gradual, with the date of the last ancient games estimated to be around the turn of the fifth century. The Greek approach to sporting festivals was only revived in 1896 when, after spending time in England and observing the growing influence of games in the public schools (*see Athleticism*), French aristocrat Baron de Coubertin instigated the modern Olympic Games.

FURTHER READING

Finley, M.I., *The Ancient Greeks* (Penguin, 1963)

Finley, M. & Pleket, H., *The Olympic Games: The First Thousand Years* (Chatto and Windus, 1976)

Munrow, A.D., *Pure and Applied Gymnastics* (2nd edn, Bell, 1963)

ASSESSMENT

Assessment in schools concerns finding out about the progress that pupils are making, or have made. It is essential for effective teaching as teachers must be aware of the stage that their students have reached in order to plan and deliver the next aspects of the students' learning.

Assessment always involves making a judgement, and this is based upon an interpretation from a body of work pupils have demonstrated, and can simply range from informal praise to a formal assessment involved in the marking of examination work (Carroll, 1994). Interpretations and judgements are made against criteria and they can give information about pupils' skill, knowledge and understanding, and their learning needs (Macfadyen & Bailey, 2002).

There are a number of rationales for the use of assessment when teaching. Within the current educational climate it is deemed to be important for communication concerning the level and nature of pupils' attainment at various points in their education; for example, at the end of specific Key Stages. As student-centred learning has become more of a focus, teachers can identify individual strengths and weaknesses of students, and this will lead to more reliable information when it comes to planning for differentiation. As teachers communicate assessment information to a variety of interested parties, it is essential that teachers have an understanding of what individuals and classes have learned, and what their potential may be. Although teachers may assess pupils to inform them of their progress, this in turn can also allow the pupils to compare themselves against relevant criteria, such as GCSE expectations, and to end of Key Stage Levels requirements. This informs the pupils of what they are required to achieve in order to progress, and as a result it may also serve to motivate them. It should be added, however, that this could also de-motivate pupils (Carroll, 1994).

The types of assessment used in schools often follow opposite pairings (Carroll, 1994; Kyriacou, 1997). Some of these include internal v external (mock GCSE/A Levels v actual GCSE/A Levels); objective v subjective (fact v opinion); and process v product (grading the manner in how something was achieved v the achievement itself). However, assessment procedures in PE are generally not as simple as this, and teachers will often use a variety of assessment types, rather than one against another. The two most often referred to in the Key Stage 3 National Strategy (DfES, 2004) are formative and summative. *Formative* is when the assessment is 'ongoing' and generally takes the form of feedback that serves the dual functions of letting pupils know how they have performed a task, while helping their development, and aiding the teacher's planning for the next phase of learning. *Summative* assessment is about recording the pupils' achievement and progress, and may come from a range of formative assessments. Summative assessment tends to be reported back to interested parties, and is evident at the end of Key Stages or units of work. Formative assessment is also used in the setting of targets that can highlight predicted grades, which are useful with examination classes, or for an end of Key Stage statement that the pupil is working towards.

Carroll (1994) outlines three other types of assessment common in schools. *Norm referenced* is where pupils are assessed in relation to each other. A good example of this is at the end of a Key Stage, and at GCSE and A Level, as they allow for comparison across wide ranges of pupils. *Ipsative referenced* assessment compares current performance with previous performance, and is useful in allowing teachers, pupils and parents to determine what progress has been made, over specific periods of time. *Criterion referenced* assessment is when pupils are assessed against specific objectives or criteria, and allows for specific grades or scores to be given in relation to the criteria.

With the Office for Standards in Education (Ofsted) becoming more focused upon child-centred learning, teachers are now using other strategies such as *self* and *peer* assessment as part of their pupils' learning. This allows for more holistic learning to take place, and gives the teacher a role more akin to that of a facilitator or advisor. The assessment that the teacher in this situation would make would be on the pupils' ability to either self or peer assess, and relates to the concept of educating the whole child in PE, and not just in the performance of an activity.

Assessment for learning refers to teachers communicating feedback through formative assessments on tasks that are a learning experience in themselves and thus provides information which allows pupils to learn and develop at their own rate (Hay in Kirk et al., 2006). This places the pupils and teachers together as part of the learning experience, and enables children to take on greater responsibility for their own development by setting their own negotiated targets.

PE can be a difficult subject for effective assessment. Indeed, an important question that can be asked is what does the PE teacher need to be assessing? If the focus is upon assessing the performance of skills, it can be difficult to ensure that everyone in large classes has been given an opportunity to perform. The context in which the skill has been revealed also needs to be taken into account. The fact that motor skills tend to be observable should make this part of the teacher's role easier, but the skill may be performed quickly, and as a result may be missed by the teacher. Assessing pupils' ability in social and affective skills is more difficult, as these aspects are not as easy to quantify as observable behaviour. This requires an experienced interpretation, usually one born out of many years spent working with children. Therefore the teacher may be required to have criteria in place so that both the pupils and less experienced colleagues have knowledge of this, to allow these types of assessment to be undertaken successfully.

The teaching position taken by the teacher should allow them to assess pupil performance without compromising their ability to manage the class. They may have to think about where they stand in relation to the performance to best observe it and to make a judgement on it. For matter of assessing social and affective issues, simply speaking to the pupils and using question and answer techniques may establish whether learning has taken place. Planning to incorporate assessment into the lesson will help structure it appropriately, and ensure that it is not a bolt-on activity.

FURTHER READING

Carroll, B., *Assessment in Physical Education: A Teacher's Guide to the Issues* (RoutledgeFalmer, 1994)

Hay, P., 'Assessment for Learning in Physical Education' in Kirk, D., Macdonald, D. & O'Sullivan, M., *The Handbook of Physical Education* (Sage, 2006), pp. 312–325

ATHLETICISM

The process in English public schools from 1860 onwards whereby sport and games were used to counteract the temptation for boys to misbehave in their leisure time and also to instil a set of values designed to create the future leaders in society. Although games were closely associated with Dr Arnold, headmaster at Rugby School (1828–1842) and his desire to achieve social control, it is unlikely that he took any personal interest in games himself. However, he undoubtedly saw their value as a means of acquiring loyalty, courage and teamwork skills and learning the importance of fair play. Arnold was keen to promote the values of the new bourgeoisie (middle classes) – primarily educated males who assumed positions of new-found responsibility as managers within industry. Characteristics including valour, honesty and endeavour were seen as an antidote to the perceived greed and vulgarity of those landowners who had become indus-trialists. Aristocratic domination was to be replaced by the bourgeois gentlemanly approach. Furthermore, Holt (1989) believes that the desire to develop future healthy young leaders reared on principles of honour and integrity also reflected the Victorian view of masculinity.

The amalgam of games that the boys themselves brought with them to the public schools started to develop rules and existing facilities were adapted; for example, an open expanse of grass at Rugby School called the Close for cricket, and the quad at Charterhouse for a dribbling version of football as opposed to the handling version.

House matches began, with sixth-form pupils assuming important roles of leadership. Fields of play developed with set boundaries and inter-school fixtures were started. Progress was rapid and some schools prioritised games

a

over academia. Professional coaches were hired, a legacy that lasts to this day in some public schools. Thus, the suggestion that games could be used to provide a worthwhile distraction from studies was seen by some masters as a process that was being taken too far and, for many, athleticism assumed cult status.

Arnold's elevation of games to the spiritual plane, that is the idea of playing sport as a means of glorifying God, led to the notion of Muscular Christianity. This was a philosophy of character developed from athleticism, again with the suggestion that a more temperate set of values could be used to counteract the excesses of the ruling class and the avarice of industrialists in particular. Perpetuated by proponents such as Charles Kingsley and Thomas Hughes, the whole process later became embedded in public schools to the extent that Mangan (in Kirk, 1992, p. 89) refers to it as a 'cultural hegemonic process at work'. This is the idea that the future leaders of society were grounded in an ideology which would maintain wealth and privilege over those subordinate classes they found themselves in authority over through education, industry and the church. Tranter's 'social diffusionist model' (1998) concurs with this, whereby the ideas and values of the dominant classes in society would filter down to the working classes through the playing of sport.

FURTHER READING
Holt, R., *Sport and the British* (Clarendon Press, 1989)

Mangan, J.A., *Athleticism in the Victorian and Edwardian Public School* (Cass, 2000)

BEHAVIOURISM

Behaviourism is linked to epistemology (the study of knowledge) and deals with the psychological theory of how learning takes place. It was viewed as the main form of learning taking place in schools for much of the 20th century, and its influence can be linked to the conditioning work of B.F. Skinner who applied punishment and rewards to modify the behaviour of rats and pigeons – a process which was then likened to that of human beings. A behaviourist theory of learning has its roots in two types of conditioning: classical, where a stimulus produces a conditioned response, and operant, where behaviour is rewarded in the expectation that it will be repeated (Macdonald, 2004). Punishment can also be used to shape the expected response to try to avoid repetition of the behaviour. Therefore, reward and punishment reinforce the behaviours for appropriate learning to take place;

Behaviourists agree that human learning is determined primarily by the environment and has grown out of the tradition that knowledge of the natural world derived from the senses can lead to rational thought and understanding.
(Macdonald in Wright et al., 2004, p. 17)

b

The knowledge is 'out there' to be learned, and this style suggests that pupils will develop the information step by step, and it will be shaped by the learning environment. When learning has taken place, it will be observable in pupils displaying the correct responses. This type of learning environment is evident in the structure of many schools within a pastoral system that rewards and punishes pupils for certain types of behaviours.

In PE a behaviourist theory of learning is commonly linked to didactic teacher-led learning (Rink, 2001). It doesn't take into account 'thinking' and instead focuses upon observable behaviours such as movement and 'cause and effect', where feedback is given to reward or to change the behaviours (Light, 2008). These instruction strategies place an emphasis on pupils learning physical motor skills with a focus on observable movement as the product. This is more apparent in sport-orientated coaching sessions as the coach is primarily concerned with the player's actions that will lead to a successful performance or outcome. Therefore, less importance is placed upon the process elements of affective and cognitive function that are synonymous with physical education;

Motor skill practice that does not require a high level of student processing may not be the best practice that we can offer, suggesting that rote repetition of responses is not appropriate practice.

(Rink, 2001, p. 116)

The teaching strategies that are usually evident in behaviourist learning will be linked to command and practice styles at the top end of Mosston & Ashworth's Teaching Spectrum (a continuum that allows teachers to choose from a range of teaching styles that move from exclusively teacher led to exclusively pupil centred). These practical teaching sessions include the regular repetition of drills practised to develop specific motor skills. A teacher's rationale for this type of learning would be that these skills are necessary in order to play a game competently. The acquisition of skills, then, would be deemed more important to the success of pupils participating, rather than the understanding of the strategies used to play the game. This type of learning does have a place in PE, as sometimes the teacher's objectives or outcomes will be skill focused. Younger players with little experience of game skills may need opportunities to practise and develop these skills to ensure that the game will not break down. The development of adequate techniques can often be a safety requirement for the activity, and mastering these will be a necessity for pupils as they will be unable to progress on to the next level without them.

Recent curricula in PE have tried to become more pupil centred. The 2008 National Curriculum for PE (NCPE) includes the concept of creativity, and processes such as making and applying decisions in its structure. Teachers can now choose the activities pupils can undertake by tailoring a curriculum to their pupils' needs, rather than being dictated to about the activities they can deliver. This allows for greater flexibility in the activities that the pupils undertake, and in the manner in which the teachers deliver them.

Because there are so many additional factors involved in the learning process other than the teacher and the pupil, it can be difficult to assume that there are direct links between the methods of teaching and the levels of learning. In particular, the choice of a specific teaching style does not always result in a specific type of learning across the whole spectrum of students (Rink, 2001).

See also: *Constructivism, Epistemology/Ontology, Teaching Strategy*

FURTHER READING

Light, R., 'Complex Learning Theory – Its Epistemology and Its Assumptions About Learning, Implications for Physical Education', *Journal of Teaching in Physical Education*, 27 (2008), pp. 21–37

Macdonald, D., 'Understanding Learning in Physical Education' in Wright, J., Macdonald, D. & Burrows, L., eds., *Critical Inquiry and Problem Solving in Physical Education* (Routledge, 2004), pp. 16–29

CLASSROOM CLIMATE

A positive classroom climate is an environment that is conducive to pupils' learning. From a PE perspective, this may be out on the sports field, in the gymnasium or in a classroom for theory-based learning. It has a purposeful atmosphere, and the teacher's authority to manage and organise the learning activities is accepted by the pupils (Kyriacou, 2007). The children are placed at the centre of the learning experience, and this positive atmosphere will influence both the motivation of the pupils and their attitudes (Mawer, 1995).

In creating a positive classroom climate, the teacher needs to set up an environment where effective learning can take place. Good & Brophy (1997) suggest three areas that will make a contribution to this. First, pupils need to feel supported by their teacher and peers, and this means that they are comfortable in making mistakes, as interactions are valued and seen as a means of learning. Second, the teacher needs to take responsibility for setting tasks that are clear and at an appropriate level of difficulty, and ensuring that these activities are meaningful and interesting. Finally, the teacher has to have high expectations of their pupils, and a sense of order present in the class, which will contribute to good behaviour and high standards. Hay & McBer (2000) found three main factors within a teacher's control that influenced pupils' progress. Thus, the teacher's professional characteristics, the teacher's skill at teaching, and the classroom climate were all aspects that determined whether classes had a positive learning atmosphere that motivated the pupils.

The hidden curriculum may well be the most important aspect of classroom climate (Kyriacou, 2007). This is what is taught implicitly by teachers, as their ideals, beliefs and actions will send out clear messages to the pupils. Therefore, the manner in which the teacher deals both with their class and within the position of a role model generally will say a lot in terms of expectations and attitudes in helping to establish a positive classroom climate. Although it may not be *as* necessary, a pleasant physical environment may have a strong influence. By ensuring that the working space is suitable for both the children being taught and the activity being delivered, health and safety matters will have also come under consideration.

Pupils in PE are perhaps more inclined to cause problems when they are not on task and therefore they need to be aware of the teacher's expectations about the work to be completed, their behaviour, and the level of effort required (Lawrence et al. in Capel, ed., 2004). Classrooms where there are routines and procedures in place, especially when they are adhered to, help in creating a positive classroom climate. Positive teaching is another contributing factor and Mawer's (1995) metaphor of the 'lighthouse effect' of keeping a wide-angled view of the class ensures that the teacher can spot problems before they arise. By praising pupils' desirable behaviours, rather than focusing upon negative aspects, the teacher is reinforcing the type of classroom that they feel is conducive to effective learning. Ultimately, however, it is the consistency of the teacher in how they approach their classes that will be a major factor in ensuring that the classroom climate stays positive.

See also: *Curriculum, Teaching Strategy*

FURTHER READING

Hay & McBer, *Research into Teacher Effectiveness,* DfEE Research Report, no. 216 (DfEE, 2000)

Lawrence, J., Capel, S. & Whitehead, M., 'Developing and Maintaining an Effective Learning Environment' in Capel, S., ed., *Learning to Teach*

Physical Education in the Secondary School: A Companion to School Experience (RoutledgeFalmer, 2004) , pp. 102–119

CLUB MARK
see Activemark

COMMUNICATION SKILLS

Communication is the process of sending and receiving information between two or more people. Rink (in Hardy and Mawer, 1999) suggested that the effectiveness of the teacher is essentially influenced by their communication skills. One of the key roles of the teacher is to impart new knowledge and transmit new information to pupils; the ability to do this successfully depends on the effectiveness of such skills. However, it is a relatively complex process and the teacher must endeavour not only to utilise the range of communication means available to them, but also to minimise the effect of conditions that interfere with the process. These skills can be considered to be both verbal and non-verbal in nature and they are used to instruct, explain, question, give feedback, motivate, reward and discipline.

Verbal communication is required in order to explain new concepts and it is important that this is done both in a concise manner and with clarity in order that pupils fully understand how to perform the skill, the context of the performance and how they might evaluate it (Mawer, 1995). Instructions and new learning points must be brief and utilise language appropriate to the age-range, development and prior learning of the pupils being taught. Similarly, specialist subject vocabulary needs to be explained. The pace of explanations is also important; it should not be rushed, for example, otherwise important information may be missed by the pupils. The voice is probably the most effective tool the teacher possesses. Variation in using the voice such as pauses, emphasis, speed, volume, pitch and tone can help reinforce the teacher's intentions (Strangwick and Zwozdiak-Myers in Capel, ed., 2004).

Non-verbal communication can be effectively used by teachers to convey feelings and responses to pupil behaviours. Facial expressions, glances and body language, for example, can be powerful tools in controlling (mis)behaviour and expressing (dis)pleasure. Eye contact, nods or a smile can all indicate that the teacher is interested in what pupils are saying. Gestures can be utilised to supplement verbal instruction in demonstrating motor skills: a 'thumbs up' can be a great morale boost for a pupil performing well, and hands can represent the action of the feet when teaching from the side of a swimming pool. Demonstration supported by brief verbal instructions can be a powerful learning tool, though Mawer (1995) suggests that the competence and status of the demonstrator and the position from which it is viewed are additional important considerations for the teacher in communicating the skill effectively. Good listening skills are another form of communication and these are important for a teacher in understanding pupil responses to questions in the formative assessment process. They are necessary when pupils are evaluating their own performance and also when listening to concerns that pupils may have (counselling role).

The factors that can interfere with the communication process between teacher and pupil include visual and auditory distractions (for example, background noise of traffic), and the distance of the teacher from the pupils. PE teachers can find the acoustics of their teaching environment challenging at the best of times (for example, playing fields, swimming pools, sports halls). Ultimately, it has been suggested that the academic performance of pupils can be determined partly by the 'audibility of teachers' (Ryan & Lucks, 2010, p. 72) and research has been recommended into the design of indoor physical education environments to improve audibility of teachers. In order to maximise pupil attention and therefore potential for learning, teachers must aim to minimise background noise when communicating with pupils; for example, by ensuring that basketballs are not being dribbled, equipment is not being moved, heaters are not blowing and pupils are not talking when key learning points and instructions are being given. Ultimately, audibility is more effective when the class are close to you, preferably in front of you. A decision needs to be made about when to bring the group together for new or reinforced instructions or teaching/learning points, as doing this too often can affect the 'flow' and pace of the lesson. Varying the volume of your voice and careful enunciation can often mean that the whole class does not have to be brought in every time you wish to speak to them, providing that pupils are quiet and attentive and movement is minimised, of course. It is important that pupils with hearing impairments are near to the teacher in these cases and that they can see you full face.

FURTHER READING

Mawer, M., *The Effective Teaching of Physical Education* (Longman, 1995)

Rink, J.E., 'Instruction from a Learning Perspective' in Hardy, C.A. & Mawer, M., eds, *Learning and Teaching in Physical Education* (Falmer, 1999)

Strangwick, R. & Zwozdiak-Myers, P., 'Communicating in PE' in Capel, S., ed., *Learning to Teach Physical Education in the Secondary School: A Companion to School Experience* (RoutledgeFalmer, 2004)

COMMUNITY SPORT

A contested area of opportunity for various interest groups, thus rendering definitions somewhat problematic. Most settings occur within the public sector and also often within the voluntary sector but infrequently in the commercial sector. They are practised using a multi-agency approach: youth and community work, social services, the probation service and education. The concept of 'community sport' developed from findings (Active People Survey, 2008/09, www.sportengland.org) which concluded that participation patterns were dominated disproportionately by the higher socio-economic social groups. By creating an emphasis on 'community' attempts have now been made to encourage participation that truly reflects the demographics of each locality.

School community sport can happen at a number of levels. Coaches from within the local area are used for both curricular and extra-curricular work, helping to create school-club links. The 'dual use' of school facilities within communities also helps with neighbourhood renewal and was one of the driving forces behind the evolution of sports colleges. The Physical Education and Sport Strategy for Young People (PESSYP) initiative has 'Club Links' as one of its ten work strands. The stated objective here is to create and develop links between schools and clubs in order that more 5–16-year-olds will participate in club sport.

Tensions involving the use of community coaches in PE lessons are also covered in other entries (*see Sports Development Officers*). Ofsted found in 2009 that the quality of delivery among coaches was not as good as among teachers due to a lack of National Curriculum knowledge and a lack of progression within lesson content. However, regarding extra-curricular involvement, Green (2008) found that when it came to fostering school-club links team sports were the most successful, with uptake most prominent from the upper primary school age group (7–10 years). Successful school participation in community sport initiatives includes involvement in Sport Action Zones (SAZs) where disadvantaged neighbourhoods are encouraged to use physical activity as a means of combating health and crime issues. Now termed Sport and Physical Activity Alliances, SAZs started as a lottery-funded initiative that acted as a localised forum for health, sport and education professionals to meet and discuss policy primarily based on distributing finance. This can lead to shared activities that transcend social and racial groupings, a community cohesion within which Benn (in Green & Hardman, eds., 2005) suggests that PE can play a vital role.

Involving a school in community sport can cause conflict. Sharing facilities and equipment can lead to vandalism, there can be difficulties allocating time slots and there can be confused expectations of costings, particularly when a school-club link is based on the premise that there is a reciprocal expectation when it comes to 'favours'. An example of this is where either the school or the club lets the other use their facilities for free in the hope that the same will be granted to them when requested. Schools should also be wary of entering into partnerships with community groups that have a conflicting agenda. This can vary from a local club's fixation with discovering talent, to commercial companies encouraging the purchasing of products that can conflict with a healthy lifestyle in order to qualify for free sports equipment. The question that needs to be answered in each case is whether interest groups are more concerned with developing sport or developing community.

Nevertheless, the fostering of links between schools and community sport groups should be seen as a positive advance for PESS. Schools can use the 'Club Mark' initiative (*see Activemark*) to investigate possibilities and also access national governing body (NGB) guidelines for successful partnerships. In general, the opportunities for increased lifelong participation and the sharing of expertise will benefit any locality and need to be part of a school's generic community programme.

See also: *Activemark, Local Management of Schools (LMS), Physical Education and Sport Strategy for Young People (PESSYP), Sports Development Officers, (SDOs)*

FURTHER READING
Green, K., *Understanding Physical Education* (Sage, 2008)

COMPETITION MANAGERS
Public Service Agreement 22 (*see Public Service Agreement*) concerns itself with the delivery of a successful London 2012 Olympic and Paralympic Games, prioritising and ensuring that opportunities are provided to inspire more children and young people to take part in competitive sport. In working towards this there has been a substantial focus on the re-introduction of competitive sport to schools. Part of the PESSYP initiative has allowed for the expansion of competition managers who work within School Sport Partnerships (SSPs). Competition managers are asked to coordinate competitive school sport within and across SSPs, ensuring that they follow the National Competition Framework. They are responsible for the planning, management and implementation of school competitions, which often link up with tournaments run by NGBs. To be an effective competition manager, liaison with partnership development managers (PDMs), school sports coordinators (SSCOs), primary link teachers (PLTs), NGBs and County Sports Partnerships (CSPs) is vital.

A research group called Loughborough Partnership (2009) found that three quarters of all SSPs have a competition manager. In addition, it was also found that most PDMs, SSCOs and PLTs believe this role is having a positive impact on the quality and quantity of competitive sport in both secondary schools and primary schools. However, given the fact that this is a relatively new role the same source has suggested that more research is required to fully assess its impact.

See also: *Physical Education and Sport Strategy for Young People (PESSYP), Public Service Agreement (PSA)*

FURTHER READING
www.youthsporttrust.org

CONSTRUCTIVISM
Constructivism is a psychological theory (or theories) of learning linked to epistemology, concerned with investigating how knowledge is formed.

Unlike behaviourist theories (*see Behaviourism*), which see knowledge as something that is 'out there' to be acquired, constructivist theory deals with the active role that learners play in their own learning. Learners make use of prior knowledge and experience to construct understanding, and the learning process is actively controlled by the learner as they build unique mental representations shaped by their own personal perceptions (Macdonald in Wright et al., eds., 2004);

A constructivist view of learning sees it as a process of adapting to and fitting into a constantly changing world. Understanding thus arises from the learner's engagement in the world through perception, motor action, and bodily senses.
(Light, 2008, p. 23)

This holistic view of learning is based upon the idea that information is processed from a higher perspective, and therefore constructivist learners will learn more and to a deeper level than those from a behaviourist perspective (Rink, 2001).

There are arguably several constructivist-type theories of learning, but Light (2008) highlights two main areas. First, there is the belief that individuals construct unique knowledge through interaction with their previous knowledge, and Piaget's theories of assimilation and accommodation are widely cited. These theories outline that individuals construct knowledge internally by adding new knowledge to previous knowledge (assimilation) and then change their knowledge based upon this (accommodation). Piaget (a Swiss psychologist and philosopher) also stated that he believed learning took place in stages during a child's development, and the four Key Stages of learning evident in the National Curriculum may have their roots in this theory. The second type of constructivism is recognised as having social aspects;

Most learning theories have assumed that learning is a private experience: groups do not learn, individuals do. Social constructivists would say that all learning is social, meaning that learning is socially constructed.
(Rink, 2001, p. 122)

Both Vygotsky (a Russian psychologist) and then Bruner (an American psychologist) have been credited with developing Piaget's theory. Vygotsky included social and cultural aspects as being the key to learning taking place, as he believed children learn better when interacting with others, especially those with more knowledge or experience. By refining thinking, using peers and competent others, Vygotsky felt that the learning that emerged from social interaction was better than learning as an individual. He believed that learners already start from a distinct knowledge base that they are often unaware of (Light, 2008), and identified the zone of proximal development as an area of knowledge between what the learner could do unassisted and assisted (Moore, 2000). Thus, the teacher would take on the role of 'scaffolding' the pupil's learning through interaction. So, by interacting with others, learners are refining their thinking (Rovegno & Dolly in Kirk at al., eds., 2006), gaining understanding, and therefore learning at a higher level.

In PE, behaviourist and constructivist ideals are often linked to styles of teaching. Most teaching methods fall under a continuum of two orientations of instruction. Indirect teaching or constructivist-style lessons are often presented as a 'big picture' that can be broken down into smaller parts. This links well with process-based 'games craft' models of teaching, and contrasts with the more direct teaching taking place in behaviourist lessons, which often focus on building up 'small chunks' to create a big picture (Rink, 2001). It may be appropriate for the teacher to start with an opposed practice situation and look at developing aspects of 'game play' rather than a specific skill that would be used in the game situation. The objective of developing strategies for success could then be applied to a variety of similar activities, rather than the teacher focusing upon skills specific to one particular game. There are several recognised models of teaching PE that develop this. These include *Teaching Games for Understanding* (Bunker & Thorpe, 1982), *Sport Education* (Siedentop, 1994) and interpretations of Lave & Wenger's (1991) *Situated Learning in a PE Context*. These models focus upon pupils constructing their own knowledge of how to play games, although the skills required to play them can be developed through the lessons.

While indirect styles of teaching and student-centred learning models are widely cited as constructivist teaching approaches, it is important to state that theories of learning are not a prescriptive set of instructional approaches (Rovegno & Dolly in Kirk et al., eds., 2006). This is because it cannot be assumed that due to a particular type of teaching taking place, a certain type of learning will follow. However, a constructivist approach does allow for the teacher to adapt their teaching to the learner's perspective, and teach what they have in front of them. The role of the constructivist teacher is to focus upon a learner's previous experiences by allowing them to explore, set and solve problems and then give pupils time to reflect and think critically on their decisions. There is often the misconception when thinking about constructivism that all decisions are down to the students. This has led to a criticism of constructivist teaching as it could undermine the role of the PE teacher; but this does not have to be the case. By taking on the role of a 'scaffolder', the teacher gives guidance to learners, allowing them to reach the intended outcomes. Therefore, a teacher is important as they are the personnel who build the environment that leads in turn to the learning (Macdonald in Wright et al., eds., 2004). Some pupils will require more support than others in understanding a concept or developing a skill; the teacher needs to have knowledge of their pupils in order to ascertain the level of support that the pupil will need, and at what point they can begin to withdraw their support.

According to Azzarito and Ennis (2003), an advantage of constructivist teaching is that it allows students to link learning to their own lives, making it more meaningful. PE is a subject that educates children beyond the physical. By seeking to develop individuals holistically through physical activities, the PE teacher can then make a lifelong impact upon the lives of their pupils.

See also: *Behaviourism, Epistemology/Ontology, Sport Education , Teaching Strategy*

FURTHER READING

Light, R., 'Complex Learning Theory – Its Epistemology and Its Assumptions About Learning, Implications for Physical Education', *Journal of Teaching in Physical Education*, 27 (2008), pp. 21–37

Macdonald, D., 'Understanding Learning in Physical Education' in Wright, J., Macdonald, D. & Burrows, L., eds., *Critical Inquiry and Problem Solving in Physical Education* (Routledge, 2004), pp. 16–29

Rovegno, I. & Dolly, J., 'Constructivist Perspectives on Learning' in Kirk, D., Macdonald, D. & O'Sullivan, M., eds., *The Handbook of Physical Education* (Sage, 2006), pp. 242–261

CONTINUING PROFESSIONAL DEVELOPMENT (CPD)

In-service training for teachers that has developed into a systematic programme with opportunities for professional accreditation. A broad definition of CPD is 'all types of professional learning undertaken by teachers beyond the initial point of training' (Craft in Armour & Yelling, 2004, p. 96). Within PE itself one of the first coordinated national initiatives came with 'Coaching for Teachers', which was introduced in 1995 as part of the National Junior Sports Programme. Run by NGBs the aim was to develop teacher knowledge and understanding of specific sports in a series of training days at a local sporting venue during the school day. This is in contrast with most opportunities to gain coaching awards, which often take place at weekends or during school holidays. MacPhail & Kirk (2001) found that this particular initiative increased teacher's confidence with the promise of free resources in the form of sports equipment as an incentive to participate. There was also a call for future training programmes to be based on the school site rather than at external venues, an outcome which has happened gradually rather than immediately.

However, despite this optimistic research concern has been expressed over the quality of professional learning opportunities (Armour & Yelling, 2002; Keay in Keay & Lloyd, 2006). PE teachers have complained that CPD does not match up to expectations; they suggest that it is dominated by theory, presenters lack knowledge, there is little time for networking and venues are geographically unsuitable. More recent developments in CPD indicate a shift towards teachers and schools taking control of their own training needs. The PE profession in particular aims to assume full responsibility for colleagues by setting up standards and examples of good practice for others to follow. As a result the Professional Development Board for PE (PDB-PE) was set up in 2001 with initial funding provided by the government. This has been superseded by the National College launched by AfPE in 2006. The aim here is to make training available for PE professionals by accredited fellow practitioners in PESS as one of the ten strands within the PESSYP initiative. Some of the topics currently available include health and safety, assessment, curriculum matters, health, leadership and school self-review. Participation and attendance within this form of CPD can lead to possible accreditation at Masters level. The overall objective is to comply with a national CPD programme that has plans based on three priorities: KS 1, KS 4 and newly qualified teachers (NQTs), deemed to be areas of comparative weakness in PE. These emanate from the National PE and School Sport Professional Development Programme managed by a consortium consisting of input from AfPE, Youth Sport Trust (YST) and Sports Coach UK (SCUK).

Armour (2006) suggests that if teachers ignore opportunities for CPD then both career development and personal effectiveness may suffer. Yet research has shown that PE teachers place a high value on informal learning from each other, a process that is unplanned and unregulated (Armour & Yelling, 2004). This could be the reason why PE teachers react with some scepticism concerning opportunities for CPD. The process involved here is a form of socialisation, which suggests to teachers that to learn from one's colleagues while working at the same time is the norm. The challenge then must be to offer CPD that is professional, relevant and well delivered.

See also: *Physical Education and Sport Strategy for Young People (PESSYP)*

FURTHER READING
Keay, J. & Lloyd, C., 'Quality Professional Development: Improving the Quality of Professional Development for Physical Education and School Sport Professionals', *Physical Education Matters,* 1 (2) (2006), pp. 20–23

MacPhail, A. & Kirk, D., 'Coaching for Teachers: An Evaluation of the Programme in Leicestershire', *British Journal of Physical Education,* 32 (2) (2001), pp. 45–48

COUNTY SPORTS PARTNERSHIPS (CSPS)
These bodies act as a link between the national strategy for sport and local delivery. CSPs are part of a government desire for 'joined-up thinking', whereby they act as a forum for local authorities (LAs), NGBs and SSPs to come together and discuss Sport England objectives. To this end they are part of a hierarchical plan to effectively implement sport policy as outlined in 'Game Plan' (DCMS, 2002).

By 2008, CSPs had begun to take on a more prominent role in strategy by assuming the powers of Sport England (*see separate entry*) regional bodies. They are there to develop and maintain local networks utilising the New Labour ideal of community partnerships. Each CSP receives

£200,000 from Sport England for two years with specific localised work programmes to be agreed between the two bodies. One example of this would be the relationship between CSPs and NGBs, whereby the former offer to both collect data and give advice on funding opportunities for clubs. In this instance they can also forge links with LAs and sports development officers (SDOs) to enable a successful application to take place. CSPs can also coordinate courses for coaches and helpers. Within schools CSPs are vital in supporting PESSYP and the 'five-hour offer' in particular. It is this central aspect of the initiative which encourages primary and secondary schools to provide both two hours curriculum PE and three hours extra-curricular school sport per week per child. CSPs have been given the responsibility for delivering the 'Extending Activities' work strand within PESSYP in addition to maintaining an input for pupil leadership and volunteering opportunities through the 'Step into Sport' programme. It is the former programme which is yet another example of partnership working, this time specifically between CSPs and SSPs. The aim is to encourage and develop identified groups among young people for even greater involvement in sport and by so doing comple-ment the National Curriculum and Every Child Matters (*see separate entries*) agenda. It is the so-called 'semi-sporty' group of young people that is targeted; those 11–19-year-olds who currently engage in two to three hours sport per week but who will need additional encouragement to reach five hours. This support will take the form of listening to young people and acting upon what they want, whether it be arranging new activities or providing new facilities. In particular, CSPs will be asked to locate providers, often in the form of local sports clubs, who will offer high quality and sustainable programmes. The target figure is for some 900,000 young people to take part in sport over a three-year period from 2008 to 2011.

At this early stage it is difficult to assess the impact of CSPs. They are part of an attempt by Sport England to minimise confusion concerning sports policy, although success is based on how well different agen-cies can work together (Robson in Hylton & Bramham, eds., 2008). However, the move towards a more defined, layered structure for 'joined-up thinking' is one that is to be applauded. Indeed, their potential for impact is such that CSPs will be 'pivotal in connecting all the pieces of the sporting puzzle' (Jackson, cited in Hylton & Braham, eds., 2008, p. 36).

See also: *Sports Development Officers (SDOS), Sport England, Physical Education and Sport Strategy for Young People (PESSYP)*

FURTHER READING
Hylton, K. & Bramham, P., eds., *Sports Development; Policy, Process and Practice* (2nd edn, Routledge, 2008)

www.sportengland.org

CULTURE
PE has often divided opinion in terms of its cultural worth and purpose (Saunders, 1982). For some it is seen as a non-intellectual pursuit beneath other studies, a form of social training which can provide relief from academia. This is in contrast to the view of educationalists who interpret PE as an important means of reflecting cultural practices through sport (Siedentop, D. et al., 1994). Saunders (1982) suggests that this difference in opinion can have implications for the curriculum in terms of whether competition is used to emphasise differences between people or whether self-worth is recognised through the promotion of more individual activities such as dance and gym. These issues can also be reflected through the issue of breadth and depth on the curriculum and just how much credence is given to pupil choice in activities. Perhaps even more crucially, cultural interpretations can influence teaching styles, including whether they are subject or child centred. Interestingly, Saunders (1982) saw Initial Teacher Education (ITE) courses as key to forming future cultural attitudes towards PE.

The cultural impact PE has on children can be interpreted differently according to personal philosophical and theoretical standpoints. For those who see the subject as relief from academia, PE can be used to move away from competitive curriculum ideology and so save some pupils from exposure to more possible failure. In this respect PE can be presented as a subject for the underachiever, a safe haven from testing and an introduction to the world of leisure (Hargreaves, 1986). Alternatively, a more competitive, elitist approach can tie in with the trends of consumer culture, particularly concerning body image (ibid.). PE teachers themselves by the very nature of their often unique relationship with students could be seen as invading pupil culture. The potential for play, fun, shared physical work and bodily contact in a variety of settings offers opportunities to build relationships using many of the characteristics of youth culture such as energy and group identity (ibid.).

However, the potential to unify will not appeal to everyone. Willis (in Hargreaves, 1986) claimed to have identified a sort of counter culture among working-class boys in the form of a reaction against organised school sport. In particular, he highlighted a division within this group based on academic ability, in that the more able were keener to participate than the less able. Within British Afro-Caribbean cultures, too, PE has histori-cally caused division, with a teacher's hope to encourage competitive school sport often conflicting with the desire for higher academic standards set by West Indian parents. Hargreaves (1986) also believes that this encourage-ment of young black males has alienated some white working-class boys. There has been very little recent research concerning the cultural experi-ences of black children in PESS (Benn in Green & Hardman, eds., 2005). Instead, the focus has concentrated more on those pupils of Asian heritage and issues concerning participation particularly with regard to the wearing of specific sports kit. One of the more interesting studies, however, looked at attitudes towards PESS held by boys from Asian communities in the north-west of England (McGuire & Collins, 1998). Research here found that the parental influence was sufficient for the subject to be afforded low status particularly when compared to other subjects perceived to be more important for offering better career prospects.

In fact, just how much recognition do PE teachers afford to cultural differences? Are stereotypes still prevalent? Moreover, does the desire to achieve in PE override the need to include? More research is required.

See also: *Discourse*

FURTHER READING

Hargreaves, J., ed., *Sport, Culture and Ideology* (Routledge and Kegan Paul, 1982)

Hargreaves, J., *Sport, Power and Culture: A Social and Historical Analysis of Popular Sports in Britain* (Polity Press, 1986)

Saunders, E., 'Sport, Culture and Physical Education', *PE Review,* 5 (1) (1982), pp. 4–15

CURRICULUM

This has often been mistaken for meaning the same as a syllabus (Ramsden, 2003). If the syllabus is the content that teachers have to teach to their pupils (NCPE/GCSE/A Level), this may create the perception that it is a simple body of knowledge transmitted from the teacher to the pupil. However, this definition limits the teacher's planning to that of content and transmission, and doesn't take into account pupils' levels of understanding and development of skills. Kelly (2004) believes that the curriculum is a sum total of the experiences that pupils have as a result of provision that is made by a school. This therefore includes the teacher's planning, their objectives and outcomes, and the resources that are used. It also takes into account the teacher's (and the syllabi's) intentions, as well as the design. These, incorporated with the teacher's delivery, form a more holistic definition of curriculum.

Schiro (2008) offers four ideologies on what the intended outcome of a curriculum may be. These explain how a curriculum fits into current educational practice depending upon the teacher's priorities for teaching, and their pupils' learning, as follows:

1 **Scholar/Academic approach:** where knowledge is passed on in a hierarchical manner and could be demonstrated by teachers with a behaviourist philosophy of teaching, and delivered using didactic teaching strategies.
2 **Social efficiency:** which schools students for roles in society; here the focus is upon the development of skills to fill needs in society, and would be evident in more vocational aspects of education.
3 **Learner centred:** focuses upon developing the individual needs of the pupil, and can be linked to constructivist approaches to learning.
4 **Social reconstruction:** educates pupils from a social perspective, where they can be schooled to develop and improve society. This aspect could have a moral component that other ideologies or curriculum definitions fail to take into account.

Although teachers may have a preferred philosophy when it comes to curriculum delivery, they could draw on different aspects of Schiro's model on appropriate occasions.

If the definition of curriculum extends beyond a transmitted body of knowledge, then it cannot be shaped by one person. The actual content being taught will come from different bodies such as the National Curriculum for Physical Education (NCPE), and different examination

C

syllabi. The teacher will have specific delivery time allocated, as well as varying levels of facilities and resources. This will often dictate the manner in which the content is delivered, as well as being influenced by the teacher's philosophy of teaching. These should all come together to ensure that the aims and the purpose of the curriculum are met – this being that the children are physically educated.

The issue of time allocated for the delivery of PE in schools needs to be considered within this context. Although it is a statutory subject as part of a school curriculum, there are no time limits, and these do vary from school to school. Indeed, they will often vary throughout Key Stages within a school, particularly as examination subjects will tend to gain a percentage of curriculum time from core PE. Although not part of a formal school curriculum, extra-curricular activities also give pupils opportunities that meet the aims and purposes of a physical education curriculum. Political influence has helped to shape a physical education curriculum with Physical Education and School Sport Club Links (PESSCL) and Physical Education and Sport Strategy for Young People (PESSYP) strategies working towards an aspiration of pupils participating in five hours of PESS per week. The fact that three of these would more than likely be out of lesson time demonstrates the importance of a school's extra-curricular programme. However, the reliance on after school sport often puts more pressure on PE teachers (Green, 2008), and this creates the issue of external providers making up the shortfall.

NCPE (1992) placed more of a focus on what constitutes a physical education curriculum. Although it gives an indication of the content that the teacher should cover, it doesn't outline the way in which it should be delivered or the resources that should be used. Ironically, subsequent changes made to the National Curriculum have given teachers more control of how they can construct a PE programme by offering greater choice and flexibility of activities. The NCPE (2008) has removed the six specific study activity areas (athletics, dance, games, gymnastics, outdoor and adventurous activities (OAA) and swimming), and this allows teachers to choose the most appropriate activities for their pupils and the school while still meeting statutory requirements.

The PE curriculum may help shape pupils' values by the ways in which the teacher, the department or the school behaves (Laker, 2000). This implies that a curriculum has a responsibility to promote and encourage socially acceptable ways of behaving as schooling can be a powerful mechanism for implicitly passing on ideals and beliefs to children (Bain, 2009). Therefore, it will be subject to a number of different aspects and ideologies that may be conflicting, and a PE curriculum will have to take these into account. The ethos of the school and personal teaching philosophies of the teachers will contribute to shaping the PE curriculum, and the location and resources of the school will play their part. Meighan and Harber (2007) present these ideologies as a continuum that range from the classroom to the institution, and continue through to the whole education system. Ultimately, it is the PE teacher who has to construct their own curriculum within these constraints.

See also: *National Curriculum, Philosophy of Teaching, Physical Education and Sport Strategy for Young People* (PESSYP)

FURTHER READING

Laker, A., *Beyond the Boundaries of Physical Education: Educating Young People for Citizenship and Social Responsibility* (RoutledgeFalmer, 2000)

Schiro, M., *Curriculum Theory: Conflicting Visions and Enduring Concerns* (Sage, 2008)

DANCE

see Expressive Movement

DIFFERENTIATION

Perhaps one of the most vital, if not one of the hardest, skills for a teacher to acquire. There is a need to first recognise and then employ a number of different strategies and methods to meet the varying needs of any group of pupils. The end product in any differentiated classroom is to work towards each student maximising their potential for growth and achievement.

The three main approaches to differentiation in PE are those of task, outcome and support:

1 **Differentiation by task** involves the teacher presenting a number of situations, which pupils can then select, or be guided to, appropriate for the ability of the learner. So in the teaching of a discus throw within athletics, for example, the task set can vary according to the ability of the pupil. Those already at a higher level can perform using the full two turns while the less able can concentrate on a standing throw.

2 **Differentiation by outcome** involves the teacher creating a challenge for an end product, which again will be set according to the students' aptitude. Macfadyen and Bailey (2002) suggest that this approach works particularly well with talented pupils. This is particularly appropriate for shooting activities in games skills where the more able are expected to aim for a higher success rate.

3 **Differentiation by support** relies on the organisational skills of a teacher reflecting ability grouping, roles and even the teaching space involved. The involvement of other personnel such as teaching assistants is also vital here.

As with many other teaching skills, differentiation does not exist in isolation. To fully maximise the differing learning needs of pupils, planning (*see separate entry*) is essential, particularly with regard to prior knowledge of ability, learning styles and, importantly, resources. So, any teacher faced with the prospect of taking on a new class should engage in dialogue with the existing teacher, consult records and observe lessons. There also needs to be an acknowledgement of differences in culture (*see separate entry*), expectation and knowledge if the teacher is to fully understand the needs of all pupils. Once teaching has commenced and relationships are established there may be a need for differentiated forms of assessment perhaps based on the varied learning styles of the pupils. This may be particularly pertinent for those students who have special educational needs. In fact, Mawer (in Hardy & Mawer, eds., 1999) states that while differentiated teaching approaches are important, the greater priority is to recognise the pupil's learning style (*see separate entry*).

After early concern by Ofsted (1995) that differentiation in many schools was a weakness, matters have improved somewhat (Ofsted, 2009). Although Macfadyen and Bailey (2002) report that this is still a cause for concern with newly qualified teachers who lack experience, Turner (in Capel et al., eds., 2003) argues that the current emphasis on target setting should aid teachers with providing the raw data necessary for the whole process. However, this would seem to contradict an earlier assertion that differentiation by individuals is almost impossible and that targeting organised groups is more workable. Whatever approach teachers may select there is no doubting Rink's (2001) assumption about the importance of differentiation: 'there may be no best way to teach, but there may be a best way to teach particular content to particular learners' (pp. 123–124).

See also: *Culture, Learning Style, Planning*

FURTHER READING
Macfadyen, T. & Bailey, R., *Teaching Physical Education 11–18* (Continuum, 2002)

d

DIPLOMAS

Introduced at Key Stage 4 (KS 4) in 2008, these new qualifications form part of the proposals for the 14–19 curriculum reforms throughout education in England and Wales. They are aimed at all levels of ability and offer flexibility for students to stay with the diplomas or progress towards other routes at the end of year 11. The three levels of foundation, higher and advanced will be available through 17 different subject areas, fully phased in by 2013. They represent a national drive to compete globally and to cater for future skill shortages. Diplomas will deliver a blend of sector and general learning within applied settings and contexts known as principal, generic and additional specialist. They are designed to provide employability for life by combining academic and vocational skills. Their design is a result of collaboration between providers and practitioners, led by employers and higher education. A significant proportion of learning will be related to employment settings with visits to the workplace or employers coming to schools.

A 'Sport and Active Leisure' diploma is due to commence in September 2010. It will comprise three elements: 'the individual', 'the industry' and 'the community'. The aims and objectives behind this course support the AfPE 'Manifesto for a World Class system of PE' (2008), which calls for three phases of learning. It is the third level at 14–19 years of age, which matches the diplomas; the manifesto calls for the teaching of 'PE life skills' comprising performance or participation, leadership, administration, officiating, academic achievement and vocational preparation. To achieve this, AfPE states that there is a need for schools to improve differentiation within lessons (*see separate entry*). At ITE level universities need to inform more about the KS 2/3 transition in PE and address the need to prepare students on how to teach life skills for when they enter the profession. It is the latter factor that will also help with the teaching of the new 'Sport and Active Leisure' diploma.

Stidder and Wallis (2006) believe that PE is well placed to embrace changes in the 14–19 curriculum and will provide a good model for other subjects to follow. Their evidence to support this statement is the growth in sports leadership (*see Leadership and Volunteering*) qualifications within PE, its recognition within the National Curriculum and subsequent preparation for higher education. Moreover, PE teachers are used to delivering a range of courses designed to meet the varied learning needs of pupils, for example GCSE, B Tec, Junior Sports Leaders Award (JSLA) and Sport Education (*see separate entry*). Such a diversity of provision reflects the principles underpinning the 14–19 curriculum reforms.

Interestingly, Stidder and Wallis (ibid.) also suggest that the new diplomas and/or other accredited courses should replace what has traditionally become known as 'core' PE, the time slot saved on the timetable at KS 4 for non-examination activities. They believe that much of the content here is outdated and fails to cater for the diverse needs and interests of pupils. Moreover, accredited courses could still transmit traditional values of PE while helping pupils prepare for an ever-changing world. Such a view is thought-provoking and certainly could be used as a bargaining tool for extra resources at this level. It is perhaps the latter factor, then, which would be the biggest concern for teachers who have consistently requested more teachers and smaller class sizes to bring PE in line with other subjects at KS 4. Perhaps such a move could be used to test whether PE really is in the ascendant within the school curriculum.

FURTHER READING

Stidder, G. & Wallis, J., 'The Place of Physical Education Within a 14–19 Curriculum: Insights and Implications for Future Practice (Part 2)', *British Journal of Teaching Physical Education* 37 (1) (2006), pp. 40–44

www.direct.gov.uk/diplomas

DISCOURSE

A simplistic definition would be to describe this term as meaning serious conversation or debate. Within PE, discourses have evolved from what are termed as 'contested areas'. These are aspects of PE teaching that have resulted in disagreements between members of the profession and sometimes resulted in 'factions' developing – small groups of people who have strong beliefs in how something should be done. Examples of this include discourse concerning gender, gymnastics and games. This in turn can create ideologies (*see separate entry*), the expression of which is developed and articulated once more through discourse (Green in Bailey & Kirk, eds., 2009).

Kirk (1992) is keen to suggest that many of the discourses found in PE have their origins in the past, but those who seek to justify the inclusion of health within PE on the basis of its inclusion in the early part of the 20th century should realise that socio-cultural factors have changed since then. So, while a large part of the contemporary justification for health-related exercise (HRE) is based on reducing future National Health bills, a hundred years ago exercise was seen as compensatory treatment for illness synonymous with deprivation.

The post-World-War-Two period is key to understanding current discourse in PE. It was a time that saw areas of contestation emerging from male PE teachers entering a profession hitherto dominated by females and produced discourse which lasts to this day; hence the continuation of discussions surrounding gymnastics, teaching styles and games, all of which have their roots in the 1940s and 1950s. Interestingly, some of the themes, even ideologies, that underpinned educational discourse at the time could be said to continue to this day, especially those of egalitarianism, social cohesion and the desire for a conflict-free society. Hargreaves (1986) even suggests that the discourses developed around PE in the post-World-War-Two period were concomitant to those used to maintain social order; that is, its justification in schools coincided with a government desire to use sport to bring society together. The aim here was to distract the nation from a realisation that Britain was losing its place as a major world power.

To suggest that teachers can become entrenched within their own discourse is to ignore the fact that colleagues can be persuaded to change their approach when given good reasons for doing so. For experienced teachers this will be a challenge and may take time. An example of this has been Information and Communication Technologies (ICT) within PE, which at various times has taken a while to embed itself within the subject (Stratton, 1999). Teachers perhaps need to step outside their own philosophies and become receptive to other ideologies (Gore in Kirk & Tinning, eds., 1990). The potential to be unleashed and the subsequent effect on pupils' learning is intriguing – ICT again being a good example of this.

See also: *Ideology*

FURTHER READING

Kirk, D., *Defining Physical Education: The Social Construction of a School Subject in Postwar Britain* (Falmer, 1992)

Kirk, D. & Tinning, R., eds., *Physical Education, Curriculum and Culture: Critical Issues in the Contemporary Crisis* (RoutledgeFalmer, 1990)

DOMAINS OF DEVELOPMENT

Introduced as an attempt to develop a taxonomy of educational objectives, the three domains are motor, cognitive and affective behaviours (Gallahue & Donnelly, 2003). Developmental PE should be sensitive to all three categories.

The motor domain is the classification for movement skill themes and is acquired through the process of motor development using fundamental movement skills (*see separate entry*). Although PE is unique in that it educates through the physical medium, it can also contribute to children's thinking skills; hence the cognitive domain. Thus, acquiring knowledge, intuition and understanding should form part of a good PE programme. This in turn will encourage both concept learning, which refers to specific areas of learning such as reasoning, and perceptual motor learning, which implies a form of sensory engagement on the part of the learner. An example of this is the use of spatial awareness within the playing of games. In fact, those responsible for developing such programmes often claim that children's cognitive functioning will be enhanced as a result, although research evidence is currently inconclusive (ibid.). However, educators do acknowledge the importance of movement to improve children's cognitive learning. By stressing the need to plan, perform and evaluate, PE teachers can therefore reinforce learning processes that are found in the classroom and challenge pupils to think through movement patterns. Indeed, the language and terminology that is used for domains of development has also often been adapted and refined for use in NCPE documents.

The affective domain refers to social and emotional development. Environmental factors and family background are important influences and the play experiences of children will be conditioned as a result. This in turn will affect personal self-esteem (*see separate entry*). Gallahue and Donnelly (2003) state that PE can play a definite role in the 'positive socialisation' of children. Thus, PE presents opportunities to develop honesty, loyalty, teamwork, self-discipline and fair play and good teachers will incorporate these into their lessons. It is this multi-faceted approach that many claim makes PE a unique subject.

FURTHER READING

Gallahue, D.L. & Donnelly, F.C., *Developmental Physical Education for all Children* (4th edn, Human Kinetics, 2003)

d

DRILL

A combination of active and rhythmic exercises usually performed from a standing position that was the main source of physical activity in state elementary schools during the latter part of the 19th century. They also made a lesser contribution to school syllabi in the first half of the 20th century. The 1870 Forster Act had attempted to create compulsory education for everyone in the form of localised school boards. It was also an opportunity for the rote learning of literacy and numeracy, which was often enforced through free-standing exercises based on children positioned between desks or, in urban areas, standing in groups of 50 or 60 on the flat roof of the school. Penn (1999) distinguishes between the drill of the 'New Imperialism' (1870–1914) and the more military style which followed at the turn of the century. The former was based on the need to keep the masses fit and alert as a means of protecting the British Empire from any perceived threat. By the 1890s this fear of attack from other nations had grown and a military theme was all pervasive, as shown by the formation of organisations such as the Salvation Army and the Church Army, who were perhaps more concerned with fighting a different type of battle altogether.

However, it was Britain's failure in the Boer War (1899–1902) which highlighted poor levels of fitness, particularly among working-class soldiers. Blame was apportioned to the elementary schools whose physical activity programme had hitherto been based upon Swedish-style drill – a rhythmic form of stretching and movement imported from the Continent. With the fear of European war looming, the Board of Education sided with the War Office to produce the 1902 Model Course. This programme of physical training based on barrack square drill was designed to improve the fitness of the working classes besides instilling discipline and obedience. Children became familiar with the use of weapons in the form of wooden staves ready for use in combat. Colonel Fox, a former inspector of Army Gymnastics, was appointed to oversee the nationwide instruction of military drill from the ages of 6 to 14 years through the use of peripatetic instructors who replaced sceptical teachers. Thus, former army sergeants were employed at the rate of sixpence per day and engaged in a command style of instruction that showed little consideration for the emotional or mental needs of children. After criticism from parents and educationalists military drill was eventually phased out of physical training syllabi by the time of World War One, although elements of other types of drill were still present right up to 1939.

See also: *Model Courses*

FURTHER READING
Penn, A., *Targeting Schools: Drill, Militarism and Imperialism* (Hodder and Stoughton, 1999)

DUTY OF CARE
Teachers have a professional obligation to ensure the welfare of the students in their charge and to see that no harm comes to them by exposing pupils to risks that can be deemed inappropriate. For PESS, this will cover not only PE lessons within the curriculum, but also out-of-school-hours education such as extra-curricular clubs and activities, sporting fixtures and trips. By law, each individual person has a responsibility to ensure that anything they do (or neglect to do) does not cause harm to another individual. Teachers, under the professional expectations placed upon them, have a duty of care to their students through Common Law, as part of their Statutory Duty of Care under the Children Act (1989) and through their Contract of Employment as set down in the Teachers' Pay and Conditions Document (for teachers in maintained schools). This latter document obliges teachers, for example, to maintain good order and discipline both in their lessons and also when engaged in extra-curricular activities.

Teachers of PE will have a greater duty of care due to the inevitably higher levels of risks to which the students are exposed in their subject area. As such, physical education teachers through their ITE, CPD and teaching experience are considered to be specialists or experts in their field.

Consequently, they are expected to make relevant informed professional judgements and take appropriate actions to safeguard the students in their care when undertaking such specialist activities in the range of teaching contexts experienced within the subject. Where this duty of care is breached and injury or damage to an individual occurs, then this could amount to negligence on the part of the teacher, though additional considerations have to be made for this to be evident. This higher duty of care means that teachers are judged against what is deemed reasonable and recommended within approved practice that is considered acceptable by their fellow professionals.

FURTHER READING

Association for Physical Education (AfPE), *Safe Practice in Physical Education and School Sport* (Coachwise, 2008)

Grayson, E., *School Sports and the Law* (Croner CCH Group Ltd, 2001)

Whitlam, P., *Case Law in Physical Education and School Sport: A Guide to Good Practice* (Coachwise, 2005)

EDUCATION REFORM ACT (ERA)

Introduced in 1988, the Education Reform Act (ERA) is often portrayed as the most important legislation to impact schools since the 1944 Butler Education Act. Although the act contained many different strands, this critique will concentrate on the two that have had the greatest impact on PE, namely the National Curriculum and local management of schools (LMS) (*see separate entry*).

The decade leading up to ERA was characterised by a growing concern over standards in schools. Prime Minister James Callaghan had highlighted problems with pupil attainment in a speech at Ruskin College, Oxford, which initiated the 'Great Debate' (1976). There was even a call for a more centralised curriculum. Once the Conservative Party under Margaret Thatcher had regained power in 1979, the debate intensified into an onslaught against teachers who were portrayed as 'trendy' idealists producing pupils who were unprepared for the workplace. This, coupled with the growing backdrop of a worsening economy and trade union disputes, made it seem as though change was inevitable.

Prime Minister Thatcher's philosophy had been heavily influenced by New Right ideology. This was a global phenomenon, a reaction to the left wing idealism of the 1970s, an amalgam of neo-liberal and neo-conservative principles. The New Right believed in combining the free market with traditional values of authority and strong leadership. Thus, an ailing public sector was subjected to the principles of market forces, a constant theme throughout ERA and specifically prevalent in the allocation of budgets as reflected in the local management of schools.

The National Curriculum itself became a government attempt to centralise control over what was being taught in schools while at the same time devolving implementation based on scant resources. PE was the last subject to be introduced, perhaps reflecting the traditional hierarchy in schools (Penny & Evans, 1999). Nevertheless, the PE profession were optimistic following a series of innovations in the 1980s that maintained the growing momentum for child-centred teaching (*see 'New' PE*). However, the construction of the NCPE and subsequent government interference proved to be a matter of expediency and pragmatism (Penny and Evans, 1999) which left many PE teachers feeling slightly disillusioned. The task of appointing membership to the NCPE working party was assigned to the Secretary of State himself. Concern was expressed at the selection of a headmaster from a leading public school as chairman and also over membership that failed to nominate a single practising PE teacher (Fox, 1992). Nevertheless, an interim report was produced that initially found favour with the PE profession, although consultation was confined to local education authorities on a limited time scale. The Secretary of State criticised the draft, generally, for containing too much 'jargon' and specifically for the assessment proposals, which were seen as being too child centred. Any attempt by the working party to discuss time allocation within the curriculum was dismissed. The revised, final document resulted in a National Curriculum for PE which led to the dominance of games and became altogether performance oriented rather than child centred. It was the former aspect which epitomised the government's attempt to restore a more 'British' curriculum and perhaps instigated subsequent attempts to 'blur' the distinction between PE and sport. Moreover, a National Curriculum had been introduced which proved difficult to implement as proved by successive alterations in 1995, 2000 and 2007.

FURTHER READING

Fox, K., 'Education for Exercise and the National Curriculum Proposals:

A Step Forwards or Backwards?', *British Journal of Physical Education*, 23 (1) (1992), pp. 8–11

Penny, D. & Evans, J., *Politics, Policy and Practice in PE* (Spon Press, 1999)

EMPLOYABILITY

This should be an important consideration for all students and trainee teachers. There is not only fierce competition for jobs but also within postgraduate ITE places in PE. However, employability is about more than *getting* a job; it is also about enhancing personal 'capabilities to operate self-sufficiently in the labour market, for example, in being able to maintain employment and have the flexibility to deal with change' (HEA/HLSTN, 2004, p. 1). Throughout a course or programme students should develop a wide range of skills to enhance job opportunities.

Employability, then, is a combination of various skills and qualities that should be developed, along with subject knowledge at any level (*see Key Skills*). Students should have covered many of these aspects within both a personal and personal development programme (PDP) and from subject-specific modules. Employability is a process; it is about being attractive to employers in terms of skills, knowledge and experience and the articulation of these (LTSN, 2002).

Enhancing employability will encompass:

- Developing subject knowledge and understanding. How do students keep up to date with developments in PE, teaching strategies, the national curriculum or with the latest government initiatives? For example, through membership of subject associations, regular reading of journals and key websites such as Qualifications and Curriculum Development Agency (QCDA) subject pages, Ofsted inspection reports, attendance at conferences and CPD courses, and contact with schools and teachers.
- Developing specific skills in relation to the teaching of PE alongside general key skills such as ICT, personal skills and communication skills.
- Drawing on experiences gained from both teaching and observations to date. What has been learned from them?
- Personal development; reflecting upon what has been achieved and how it has aided personal development. How has it informed future practice and behaviours?(*See Reflective Practice.*)

- Personal qualities; what aspects of the student's character and personality are going to impact on a future employer or postgraduate course leader? What impression will be made in interviews for example? Is there anything that the student feels should be developed in particular?

(adapted from LTSN, 2002)

Some of the skills and qualities identified by employers as being important in graduates include: motivation and enthusiasm, interpersonal skills, team working, oral communication, flexibility and adaptability, initiative, productivity, problem solving, planning and organisation, managing own development and written communication (HEA/HLSTN, 2004). PE students should find that many of these characteristics are developed automatically throughout their undergraduate course of study.

As potential teachers, students should endeavour to adopt a 'professional' approach as early as possible. Many of the skills and qualities outlined above would be part of the professional expectations within the school context. Students will need to consider what an effective professional teacher is and endeavour to adopt those qualities in order to enhance employability.

See also: *Reflective Practice*

FURTHER READING
Higher Education Academy, *Student Employability Profiles* (HEA, 2007), available to download at www.heacademy.ac.uk/resources

ENERGY SYSTEMS
In order to produce movement (mechanical energy), the muscles require a usable form of chemical energy. This chemical energy is stored in the muscle cells as a compound called adenosine triphosphate (ATP), which, as its name implies, contains three phosphate molecules with high energy bonds. When the ATP molecule is broken down (ATP-ase) and a phosphate group liberated, energy is released for muscle contraction to occur. There is not an inexhaustible supply of ATP in the muscles and it must therefore be regenerated or resynthesised if exercise is to continue. It is through the energy systems that this regeneration of ATP takes place. There are three energy systems involved in this resynthesis of ATP; the

contribution of each depends upon the extent and intensity of the exercise (energy continuum) and the availability of relevant fuels such as carbohydrate and fat. The pathways through which ATP is resynthesised (from adenosine diphosphate, ADP) involve the fuel (depending on intensity and duration) passing through enzyme-controlled reactions. Some of the processes occur aerobically (requiring oxygen) whereas others are anaerobic.

The first of these systems is the alactic energy system (ATP-PC system), which is anaerobic and involves the use of stored creatine phosphate (CP) to resynthise ATP via the enzyme creatine kinase. However, there are only sufficient CP stores for up to ten seconds of activity. This system is therefore used in activities of high intensity and short duration such as the 100m sprint.

The second anaerobic system is the lactic acid system (or anaerobic glycolysis). This involves the breakdown of stored carbohydrate (glycogen) in a series of enzyme-controlled reactions called glycolysis. Glucose (from glycogen) is broken down into pyruvic acid, which releases sufficient energy to resynthesise two molecules of ATP. Due to the lack of availability of sufficient oxygen (through high intensity exercise) at this point, pyruvic acid is converted to lactic acid, which has the effect of inhibiting the enzyme reactions in glycolysis. An 'oxygen debt' (excess post-exercise oxygen consumption – EPOC) is thereby incurred and the intensity of the exercise must be reduced or stopped. This system is used under high intensity short duration activity regimes; for example, the 400m sprint.

Where exercise is sub-maximal, such as in endurance events, the aerobic energy system can be utilised, whereby there is sufficient oxygen taken in to ensure that pyruvic acid can be broken down further to produce a higher yield of ATP. The pyruvic acid is converted to acetyl coenzyme A, which enters the Krebs (citric acid) cycle and is completely broken down to carbon dioxide and water through this and the electron transport chain (ETC). These stages take place in mitochondria within the muscle cell sarcoplasm. Fat may also be used to fuel this system under prolonged submaximal conditions via the process of beta-oxidation. The total yield of ATP molecules is 38 per glucose molecule under these aerobic conditions.

Each of the systems can be seen as part of a continuum that supplies energy in the form of ATP. The systems will contribute continuously but the extent to which they do so will be affected by the intensity and duration of the activity (see Figure E.1). Training may also aim to make use of these energy systems more efficient; for example, by delaying the

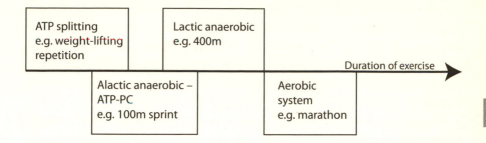

Figure E.1: The Energy Continuum

onset of blood lactate accumulation (OBLA) or anaerobic threshold. In untrained individuals this is usually between 50 to 60 per cent of their VO2 max (maximal oxygen consumption), whereas in highly trained athletes, the threshold may be around 70 to 80 per cent of their VO2 max.

FURTHER READING

Kirk, D., Cooke, C., Flintoff, A., & McKenna, J. *Key Concepts in Sport and Exercise Sciences* (Sage, 2008)

Sewell, D., Watkins, P. & Griffin, M., *Sport and Exercise Science: An Introduction* (Hodder Arnold, 2005)

EPISTEMOLOGY/ONTOLOGY

An understanding of epistemology is important for teachers as it underpins the theories behind learning, and also for researchers as it shapes the design undertaken, and guides methods used in collecting and interpreting the data. Epistemology and ontology look at that knowledge which is based upon the nature of existence, and what a person would regard as 'truth'.

Ontology is a philosophical outlook on how a person views the world, and what they know about it. Ontological assumptions are influenced by beliefs and values, and, for research purposes, form a starting point (Grix, 2002). There are two opposing positions from which to start: *objective*, where social reality is seen as external to and independent of individuals (Cohen et al., 2007), and *subjective*, where reality is seen as being socially constructed and the result of human thought (Opie, 2004). If a researcher was seeking to establish a rationale for the success of a pupil's performance in games, the objectivist would look to any physiological and genetic differences that could be identified and measured such as speed, agility, balance and stamina. The subjectivist would look at the social factors that may have contributed to their success, like opportunities to access training, the level of players that they were playing with and against, and the level of the teaching (or coaching) that they had received.

If ontology is what is out there to be known, then epistemology is the theory of how the knowledge is acquired and how we have come to know what we know. By establishing two ontological assumptions of objectivity and subjectivity, the researcher can link two epistemological paradigms in a similar way. In epistemology, objective knowledge is real, and can be captured, and as a result quantified and measured. Subjective knowledge, however, is personal, and is based upon perceptions, which require questioning those involved to gain both their opinions and their experiences, meaning measurement is more qualitative (Opie, 2004).

These approaches to learning may have implications for PE teachers in terms of how pupil learning will take place, that is the styles and strategies that the teachers will use, and of the content concerning what is to be learned. Therefore, the epistemological positions of the teachers may be apparent (subconsciously) in the beliefs that they hold about learning in PE, and in the way that they go about teaching it. If the 'knowledge' to be learned in PE is seen as being about motor behaviour and movement, the teacher may use direct styles of instruction to facilitate it taking place, as these are often seen to be effective ways of enabling pupil learning (Mawer, 1999). However, if the knowledge to be acquired is seen as being more holistic, then indirect teaching approaches may be more appropriate if there is a focus upon creativity and decision making (Macfadyen & Bailey, 2002). These would be examples of how epistemological theory underpins pupil learning (Rink, 2001).

As part of the research process, the researcher's positionality (their ontological and epistemological standpoint) would shape the direction of their intended research, as it would guide the methodological approach undertaken. Although closely matched, epistemology is shaped by ontology, and this will in turn define the type of questions that the researcher will ask and structure how they will go about answering them (Grix, 2002). If the knowledge to be acquired is 'out there' and it is hard and objective, an observer role may be best for accruing quantitative data. This will allow the researcher to quantify aspects of observed behaviour. When the knowledge or truth to be acquired is personal, subjective or unique, then the researcher will need to be personally involved with the subject(s), and interact with them in order to gain access to their beliefs, perceptions or ideas. Acknowledging an epistemological standpoint will aid novice researchers in guiding future research practice.

See also: *Behaviourism, Constructivism, Methodology, Research Approach, Research Methods (Data Collection)*

FURTHER READING

Grix, J., 'Introducing Students to the Generic Terminology of Social Research', *Politics,* 22 (3) (2002), pp. 175–86

Opie, C., *Doing Educational Research: A Guide to First Time Researchers* (Sage, 2004)

ETHICS

Undergraduate students of physical education will invariably have to undertake a small-scale research project, usually in the form of a dissertation. According to Wellington (2000), anyone who is contemplating research should put ethical issues at the forefront of conducting and presenting educational investigation. Indeed, he suggests that it should override all other considerations. If the role of the researcher is to establish 'truth' or 'social reality', then the knowledge that is discovered has the potential to affect the lives of the people involved. Therefore, the manner in which the researcher conducts the research has to be socially acceptable, and they have to balance the notion of truth with a responsibility to the rights and values of the subjects involved. Research is personal to each researcher, and this requires that every characteristic of each case needs to be considered, as any research that involves people has the potential to cause damage, no matter how unintentional it is (Opie, 2004).

Bassey (1999) outlined that there has to be respect for democracy, truth and the people involved in research. He acknowledged that there was the potential for these ideals to clash, and he drew attention to the controls of validity, reliability and informed consent to ensure that such a call for respect was observed. Furthermore, differing research bodies have produced guidelines to outline the researcher's key responsibilities.

To ensure that educational investigation is socially and morally acceptable, the British Educational Research Association (BERA) has produced a document to guide the conduct of the researcher. Thus, what constitutes harm for the subjects of educational research may be unclear, but the BERA document offers guidance about conduct across all aspects of the research process. Their aim is to:

… weigh up all aspects of the process of conducting educational research within any given context, and to reach an ethically acceptable position in which their actions are considered justifiable and sound.

(BERA, 2004)

The guidance is underpinned by principles which consider that educational research should be conducted by respecting the person; knowledge itself, democratic values, quality and academic freedom. BERA guides researchers in education by promoting this code, although it tries to avoid being too specific as it has to work within the confines of social research, where there are many different settings.

However, Wellington (2000) does identify specific areas of the research process that should be ethically sound. When designing the research project, its implications need to be considered, especially whether the particular approach or methodology is justifiable. If children are involved, then the methods employed to gather the data need to be carefully considered. Here, the researcher may be in a position of social power over the children, and this may well have an influence on the data that is collected. If the researcher is present when the data is being collected, either by questionnaire or interview, the respondents may be inclined to respond according to the way in which they think the investigator wants them to. This is why aspects like confidentiality, anonymity and the notion of informed consent are important. If the respondents filling in a questionnaire or answering questions by means of an interview feel that their opinions will reflect badly on them, or will be used against them at a later date, it will probably reflect the validity of the responses that are made. Therefore, it is important that the researcher portrays himself/herself in a manner that is impartial and free from bias. Ultimately, as the collection, collation and analysis of data can be subject to researcher bias, care will need to be taken when drawing findings or making generalisations from data obtained.

See also: *Informed Consent, Reliability/Validity, Research Methods (Data Collection)*

FURTHER READING

British Educational Research Association, *Revised Ethical Guidelines for Educational Research* (BERA, April 2004)

Wellington, J., *Educational Research: Contemporary Issues and Practical Approaches* (Continuum, 2000)

EVERY CHILD MATTERS

This is a national framework for 'joined-up' thinking on children's services coordinated by the Department for Culture, Schools and Families (DCSF). The objective is for cross collaboration between education, culture, health, social care and justice. The term 'Every Child Matters' (ECM) evolved from a government green paper of the same name that was published in 2003. A year later some of the core principles were used to underpin 'The Children's Act', which aimed to provide a clear pathway of support for children from birth to adulthood at the age of 19.

More specific support relates to what are commonly referred to as the five outcomes for ECM:

1 Be healthy
2 Stay safe
3 Enjoy and achieve
4 Make a positive contribution
5 Achieve economic well-being

The core values of ECM have been further developed by the 'Children's Plan' introduced in December 2007. This is a ten-year strategy designed to make England the best place in the world for children to live. It aims to put families at the centre of a child's development along with improving health, education, reducing offending rates and removing child poverty by 2020.

The 'Extended Schools' initiative has emerged as a by-product of the ECM agenda. This aims to place schools at the heart of communities by using them as a means of providing access to local services. By encouraging partnerships with both private and voluntary providers the government hopes to capitalise on community respect and trust for schools. Particular focus is placed on opportunities for the following:

- High quality childcare from 8 a.m. to 6 p.m.
- Extra-curricular clubs
- Parenting support
- Community access to ICT, sports, arts and adult learning facilities

Specific funding for this initiative is placed with local authorities who devolve finance as necessary. The implications for school sport funding opportunities are obvious.

Every Child Matters is frequently used as a reference point for any report on children's services. Thus, the Ofsted statement on PE in schools for 2005/08 suggests that the subject has contributed effectively to ECM outcomes, especially 'being healthy', 'enjoying and achieving' and 'making a positive contribution'. School PE departments may well wish to further investigate funding possibilities that could be accessed through 'Extended Schools' (Williams, 2009).

FURTHER READING

Office for Standards in Education (Ofsted), *Physical Education in Schools 2005/08* (Ofsted, 2009)

www.everychildmatters.gov.uk

EXAMS

The growth in both the number of PE examinations offered in secondary schools and in the statistics for pupils taking them can be traced back to the 1970s. It was at this time when an innovative approach towards assessment began with the arrival of a Certificate of Secondary Education (CSE) in PE. Because the subject was not offered at the more popular General Certificate of Education (GCE) level, its impact was limited. However, with the creation of the new General Certificate of Secondary Education (GCSE) in the 1980s, an assessment targeted at all pupils, the educational climate became conducive towards exams in subjects hitherto unrepresented at this level. In the 1990s the growth in GCSE PE gathered pace alongside developments in A level. From 2000 exams became more flexible with the arrival of a modular approach at A level and the introduction of half units at GCSE level.

The impact of examinations (300 per cent growth in GCSE PE entries and 3,000 per cent growth in A level entries between 1990 and 2006) is such that Green (2008) suggests that it has led to the most significant change in secondary school PE in the last 30 years. Moreover, there are virtually no historical precedents to underpin the idea of such formal assessments in PE, although Nutt and Clarke (in Laker, ed., 2002) believe that the educational trends over this period of time have gravitated towards the return of propositional knowledge, i.e. the mere learning of facts, as the dominant form of education in schools. Therefore, they argue that PE could not remain immune from such a move back towards the importance of exams and the technocratic model of teaching that has come with it.

Not everyone in the PE profession has welcomed these moves and the early arguments against such developments surrounded difficulties in making practical assessments, in remaining objective and in comparing activities. Individual pupil differences related to physique rather than skill were highlighted as a cause for concern. Some teachers were also initially wary of the need to become exposed to departmental scrutiny both within and between schools. The need for greater lesson preparation brought with it fears that school extra-curricular sports programmes may suffer as well. More recently, other concerns have arisen with battles over terminology (is it PE or is it sport?), and the need to accommodate other forms of accreditation as well; for example, in leadership courses such as the Junior Sports Leader Award (JSLA) (*see Leadership and Volunteering*).

However, right from the start many PE teachers saw the growth in exams as the chance to raise the subject's status and profile. Competition for more lessons on the timetable intensified after the 1988 Education Reform Act and this was the chance for PE to compete both here and for other resources. Schools also saw that the practical nature of the subject could appeal to both disaffected and less academically able pupils who, after achieving success, could then go on and apply for jobs within the ever-growing sports and leisure industry. Generally, it was perhaps this perceived need by PE teachers for improved status, not just for the subject but for their own careers as well, that underpinned this growth. Green (2001) also found that teachers welcomed the opportunities to deliver within the classroom as opposed to the more traditional PE settings. In addition they appreciated the chance for further financial gain if roles such as those of a moderator were undertaken.

The growth in exam PE has brought with it a number of problems and issues for teachers. Practical assessment can still be a problem, particularly with variables such as the weather, equipment and facilities. There is also a general concern that pupil success is achieved far too disproportionately within the practical component rather than the theoretical aspects (ibid.). Standardising both within and between schools can also be a problem. However, perhaps the biggest concern has been that the levels of uptake and success in exam PE have reflected traditional gender issues within the subject, i.e. males tend to dominate.

The growth in exam PE has reflected wider educational issues such as the drive to subject schools to market forces. Green (in Green &Hardman, eds., 2005) feels that PE teachers have reacted out of fear for both themselves and their subject. Ironically, the increased academicisation of PE has placed extra pressures on school departments just at the same time that government initiatives have called for a greater emphasis on the practical aspects of the subject to meet a number of disparate community objectives. So, currently PE teachers find themselves having to meet a number of varying demands that place strains on all aspects of their time management skills.

FURTHER READING

Green, K., 'Examinations in Physical Education: A Sociological Perspective On a "New Orthodoxy" ', *British Journal of Sociology of Education,* 22 (1) (2001), pp. 51–73

EXPRESSIVE MOVEMENT

This refers to gymnastic and dance activities within the PE curriculum. Its place and positioning has been one of the most keenly contested topics within the history of PE. It has also come to symbolise conflicts between male and female teachers while at the same time bringing to the forefront issues concerning terminology and gender representation among pupils.

Gymnastics in particular has had a major influence in shaping the course and destiny that PE has taken. Kirk (2010) builds a powerful case for the suggestion that such was its early dominance within state schools, that from 1850 to 1950 a physical-education-as-gymnastics ideology was all-pervasive. At this time, gymnastics took on a number of different guises including 'drill', 'gym' and 'physical training' (*see Drill*). The first influences came from Europe and were based on the early 19th-century ideas and practices of Friedrich Ludwig Jahn in Germany and Per Henrick Ling in Sweden. Jahn's sport-based 'Turnen' (a forerunner of what is now termed Olympic Gymnastics) was designed as an exposition of upper body strength involving the use of rings, pommel horse and bars, while Ling's methods were therapeutic, free-standing exercises linked to body development. Both had borrowed from the earlier ideas of Guts Muths, with Jahn incorporating the use of apparatus and Ling emphasising exercise based on the principles of anatomy. However, it was the Swedish methods that were eventually adopted by most state schools as shown by their appearance in the form of instructional tables as part of the 1909, 1919 and 1933 Physical Training syllabi. Kirk (2010) suggests that irrespective of whatever form was selected by schools, gymnastics represented a hegemonic attempt to keep the working classes in check. The very nature of the activity implied discipline and order: queuing in silence, standing in lines and obeying commands. There is even a suggestion that some gymnastic exercises had elements of militarist symbolism; for example, vaulting could be seen as representing horsemanship and ultimately training for the cavalry.

The role of Swedish gym in the school curriculum was eventually challenged by female gymnasts who based their work on the ideas of Laban's modern educational dance. This came to a peak in the post-World-War-Two period with a crucial collision between the three forms of gym: educational, Swedish and Olympic ('Turnen'). With the recent entry of male teachers into the PE profession, gymnastics became a strongly contested concept itself, especially with games in the ascendant. Kirk (1992) saw this as part of the need at the time for a more meritocratic society, with people desiring the freedom to express themselves and so move away from the more regimented, formal approach that some forms of gymnastics represented. This is somewhat ironic given that educational gymnastics usually provides such opportunities for child-centred teaching based on creativity and individual interpretation. However, such was the pull towards other areas of activity within state schools that Kirk (2010) sees this period of time as the start of physical-education-as-sport ideology. By the 1960s Swedish gym had all but disappeared from the curriculum. Educational gym had now become very popular in schools, particularly when taught by female teachers as a form of movement to music. Some male PE teachers did, however, maintain a preference for more formal, strength-based elements and to this day gymnastics is perhaps still used to express identities of femininity and masculinity.

The history of dance within PESS is complex, problematic and even political. As a designated National Curriculum area of activity its place and value has been recognised, but the fact that specialist teachers are often used and that it can be studied as a distinct separate subject has perhaps marginalised its true worth. In a PE curriculum still dominated by games the uptake for GCSE dance is on the increase, although the proportion of boys enrolled is as low as five per cent (Ofsted, 2009). However, the potential for dance to act as a vehicle for the promotion of inclusion and understanding now and in the future is great (Benn in Green & Hardman, eds., 2005; Laker, 2003). Indeed, it is this opportunity to represent and celebrate cultural diversity that has perhaps led to a close alliance between dance professionals and the Department for Culture, Media and Sport (DCMS), where the allocation of funding is often based on links with educational settings.

Expressive movement may not have the prominence within contemporary PE curriculums that it used to but its worth as an alternative form of less competitive activity is unrivalled. It is also a clear opportunity for teachers to engage in child-centred teaching and should be seen as a welcome addition to celebrate the unique breadth that a good PESS programme should offer.

FURTHER READING

Benn, T., 'Race and Physical Education, Sport and Dance' in Green, K. & Hardman, K., eds., *Physical Education: Essential Issues* (Sage, 2005), pp. 197–219

Kirk, D., *Defining Physical Education: The Social Construction of a School Subject in Postwar Britain* (Falmer, 1992)

FURTHER EDUCATION SPORT COORDINATORS (FESCOS)

Personnel attached to further education colleges with the aim of developing sports programmes for the 16–19 age group. Following a pilot scheme, the first FESCOs were appointed in April 2008; 190 colleges applied for the scheme with initial acceptance granted to 31 institutions. Successful applicants usually devote two days a week to the job, with the remainder of their time spent fulfilling other roles such as lecturer, coach or sports development officer (SDO).

Specific duties include interacting with partners on a number of different levels. Thus, a meeting with the local School Sport Partnership (SSP) may lead to the involvement of further education students in the organisation and running of school festivals. Liaising with County Sports Partnerships (CSPs), SDOs and Higher Education Institutions (HEIs) will help to access funding, particularly for Extending Activities projects. Within the college itself, FESCOs need to build relationships with existing staff and students to establish an identity with this role, especially when it comes to introducing new initiatives such as intra-mural competitions. The latter is an example of an activity which may arise from a 'needs analysis' undertaken with college students; this would be the first task required from any new FESCO. Finally, establishing relationships with the local sporting community may lead to enrichment programmes and club–college links in particular.

The Loughborough Partnership, a research group investigating young people in PE and sport, found in 2009 that of the first appointments to the FESCO initiative 60 per cent had worked in further education before. They faced a diverse set of challenges based on the fact that colleges varied from populations of 900 students to 22,000. The partnership found that participation levels among students were low, significantly so for females when compared to males, and that the average number of activities offered per institution was 11. However, the benefits of the initiative ascertained at this early stage included the improvement of the transition phase between school and college and the opportunities presented for introducing students to leadership and volunteering programmes. FESCOs felt that general links with schools were improving and that college enrichment programmes were developing. The key challenges for the future centred on the need to clarify job specification, especially with regard to expected roles within a local SSP. Similarly, maintaining realistic expectations is a concern along with the difficulty of measuring success given the variability in type and number of institutions.

PE and sport within the further education college setting has undergone a transformation of late. The establishment of sporting academies (*see Further Education Sporting Academies*) and the appointment of FESCOs are evidence of a concern for activity levels among the 16–19 age group. It will be interesting to see if similar attention is given towards the timetabling of PE lessons and extra-curricular opportunities for those students of a similar age who prefer to stay on at school.

See also: *Further Education Sporting Academies, Physical Education and Sport Strategy for Young People (PESSYP)*

FURTHER READING
www.lboro.ac.uk/department/ssess

www.youthsporttrust.org

FITNESS

This has many different meanings depending on the context in which it is used and the people to whom the term is referring; fitness will mean one thing to an Olympic athlete, for example, and something entirely different to a member of the general public. In the context of PESS, the specific components that comprise fitness need to be understood since they are important to varying degrees in different activities and this impacts on selection of training methods to improve those components. Fitness for hammer throwing will be necessarily different from fitness for distance running, for example. A hammer thrower needs explosive strength, whereas good cardio-respiratory fitness is a prerequisite for coping with the demands of distance running.

A much more general interpretation of fitness is that associated with everyday health and well-being as opposed to sports performance. Being able to run for a bus or reach to the top shelf in a supermarket is what some people might consider to be important in fitness. From a PESS perspective, both elements of fitness are important as teachers strive to ensure that pupils are equipped with the knowledge and understanding that will promote lifelong participation in physical activity and fitness for health, while ensuring a greater depth of understanding of the role of fitness in specific 'sports'.

Fitness can be considered from 'health-related' and 'skill-related' (or motor) perspectives. It is the health-related aspect of fitness that tends to be associated with the health and well-being of the individual. As such it encompasses components such as strength, stamina (cardio-respiratory fitness or endurance), suppleness (or flexibility) and body composition (*see Health-related Fitness*). Because of their potential to minimise the more negative health implications – for example coronary heart disease, hypertension, obesity – relevant exercise and training in these areas of fitness can help to reduce the possibility of such problems arising. In terms of sporting performance, the health-related components are of importance in that once identified as key fitness requirements of the sport, training can be made specific to those components in order to elicit physiological adaptations and optimise performance. The type of strength required for the activity – for example explosive, static, dynamic – will dictate the strength training methods and regimes required in an athlete's training programme.

f

Health-related fitness (HRF) consists of the following:

1 **Stamina:** the efficiency of the cardio-respiratory system to allow oxygen to be absorbed and transported to the working muscles to ensure that their demands can be met. This includes the efficiency with which by-products are removed from the working muscle. This underpins all aerobic-type activities and can be improved through endurance-based training methods; for example, continuous training, fartlek ('speedplay') training and variations of interval-based methods.

2 **Strength:** the total force that can be developed during a maximal voluntary muscle contraction. Static strength is that used against a relatively immovable object so that there is virtually no movement at the joint. Dynamic strength involves the repeated joint movement associated with many physical activities, whereas gross strength is the maximum force that can be exerted such as in weight lifting, where a great resistance must be overcome. Training methods such as weight training, medicine ball work, pulley work and body weight exercises as in circuit training and plyometrics can be used to develop strength.

3 **Suppleness (or flexibility):** the range of movement allowed by the joint. This is determined by the type of joint (structure), the size of the surrounding muscles and the elasticity of the surrounding connective tissues (ligaments and tendons). Suppleness can be developed through static, dynamic and passive stretching and also proprioceptive neuromuscular facilitation (PNF), a method of mobility training where the athlete performs a maximum (passive) stretch, then contraction, then further stretches the muscle, the objective being to increase the mobility range of the muscle.

4 **Body composition:** the distribution of muscle and fat when considering the physiological make-up of the body. Excessive body fat is a contributing factor in cardiovascular disease and obesity.

Skill-related fitness is associated more with the neuromuscular system and the more skills-based qualities of activities and includes:

1 **Speed:** the maximum rate at which a body or part of a body can move, e.g. arm speed in discus throwing.

2 **Agility:** the ability to change direction at speed while maintaining control, e.g. a badminton player moving on court.

3 **Balance:** maintaining equilibrium so that the centre of gravity is over the supporting base, e.g. a gymnast in a handstand position.

4 **Coordination:** the interaction of the nervous and motor systems in producing movement which is accurate, precise and effective, e.g. hand-eye coordination in a goalkeeper catching a high cross while under pressure from opposition players.

5 **Reaction time:** the time between an initiated muscle response to a given stimulus, e.g. an athlete responding to the starter's gun in a sprint race.

FURTHER READING

Kirk, D., Cooke, C., Flintoff, A. & McKenna, J., *Key Concepts in Sport and Exercise Sciences* (Sage, 2008)

FITNESS TESTING

Fitness testing involves taking measurements that help to determine the levels of fitness and health of an individual. Measurements are usually compared to standardised norms or to the individual's previous performances in the tests. Testing is an important part of regulating an athlete's training programme; for example, to establish baseline fitness measurements, to prescribe future training regimes, to monitor training effectiveness, to check if training targets are being met and for talent identification purposes. Some tests for elements of fitness require expensive specialist equipment, whereas others require little equipment at all. In most fitness testing, however, there are certain prerequisites if the tests are to be beneficial and worthwhile. It is important to know what is being tested and to ensure that the specific selected test will indeed cover that particular component of fitness. It is imperative that the protocols for the test are closely adhered to, particularly where comparisons are being made. In this case, it is important that the tests are reliable and valid and that results can be replicated. It is important, for example, that other factors are taken into consideration such as the motivation of the individual being tested. The test should be standardised so that the same conditions are applied to each individual/group and relevant variables controlled.

In terms of PE, there has been much debate about the educational value of fitness testing and its place in the school curriculum (Harris, 2000). Testing can provide measurements for fitness components in pupils as outlined above; however, the question should be for what aims and purposes? Where explanations and educational benefits are identified as part of the process within a well-planned health-related exercise programme, then testing can be beneficial, for example in identifying baseline fitness levels and using the information to devise training programmes. Testing can also be a good motivational tool for some pupils but inevitably not others who may find the whole process demeaning, embarrassing and uncomfortable (Harris 2000). Testing is not recommended for pupils of primary school age due to the different range of maturational levels of pupils, the levels of cognitive understanding of the meanings of test results and the implications of the test results. Harris (2000) recommends that time can be more effectively and beneficially spent in simple observation and monitoring of the effects of exercise at this age. It is important that, where testing does take place to support effective learning in physical education, the tests used are appropriate for the age-range and developmental maturity of the pupils; for stamina, for example, sub-maximal tests are preferred, such as appropriate low intensity step tests which look at heart-rate responses during exercise and recovery. Any tests should form part of a well-planned, well-balanced programme of health and fitness education and age-appropriate norm-based reference charts should be consulted. Regular repeated testing and using tests purely for their competitive value is not beneficial; 'administering fitness tests to gain data for records without attention to the tests' educational role is not advised' (Harris, 2000, p. 26).

It is important to remember that testing should be individualised in line with the inclusive nature of PE – using activities appropriate to the developmental age, maturity and ability of the pupil. It has also been suggested that the time spent on fitness testing within the PE curriculum may often detract from opportunities to provide health-promoting activities that would be more beneficial in developing pupil knowledge and understanding of physical fitness (Harris and Cale, 2006). Clearly, a balance needs to be sought between these two differing outcomes.

FURTHER READING

Harris, J. & Cale, L., 'A Review of Children's Fitness Testing', *European Physical Education Review,* 12 (2) (2006), pp. 201–225

Harris, J. & Cale, L., 'Fitness Testing in Physical Education: Misdirected Effort in Promoting Healthy Lifestyles in Physical Activity', *Physical Education and Sports Pedagogy,* 14 (1) (2009), pp. 89–108

FUNDAMENTAL MOVEMENT SKILLS

This is 'an organised series of basic movements that involve the combination of movement patterns of two or more body segments' (Gallahue & Donnelly, 2003, p. 52). These movement skills develop as children mature and can be applied later in a more specialised manner to a number of different sports. There are three categories of fundamental motor skills:

1 Stability, for example twisting and turning
2 Locomotor, for example running and jumping
3 Manipulative movements, for instance striking and throwing

Fundamental movement skills are usually separated into three phases: preparation, execution and recovery, i.e. the follow-through phase, for example after the execution of a striking skill (Gallahue & Donnelly, 2003).

Development of fundamental movement skills begins early when children experiment with a variety of motor tasks in a number of different environments – home, community play areas and pre-school settings. These are important foundations to build on and trends based on observation suggest that rapid early development can continue into middle childhood for some movements such as throwing. Research has focused on describing stages through which a child should progress, from an immature to a mature pattern. The rates at which children can do so will vary. A key research consideration here is the interval between experimental observations with two or three months as a suggested optimum period (Malina et al., 2004). This may have implications for testing in PE, especially when observing potential gifted and talented pupils who may be identified based on early maturation rather than potential. If testing and observation could take place more frequently, then identification could be more reliable, but finding time and space within a crowded PE curriculum could be difficult. Further research is required on the variables which occur within each stage of development in order to fully understand how children progress (ibid.).

Gender differences in the development of fundamental motor skills are pronounced. When studying the rate of attainment, boys reach each stage for overarm throwing and kicking earlier, while girls are superior for hopping and skipping (Gallahue, 2003). Differences between the sexes are most apparent for overarm throwing. The rate of development within other basic skills is fairly similar between both boys and girls, although variation is found at late childhood. Thus, girls reach the final two stages of catching earlier than boys. The testing of fundamental motor skills in young children remains problematic since scores vary considerably from one occasion to the next due to issues concerning motivation, cooperation, maturation and changes in body size and proportions (Malina et al., 2004). Again, research such as this should be borne in mind by physical educationists when engaging in the assessment of children.

FURTHER READING
Gallahue, D.L. & Donnelly, F.C., *Developmental Physical Education for all Children* (4th edn, Human Kinetics, 2003)

Malina, R., Bouchard, C. & Bar-Or, O., *Growth, Maturation and Physical Activity* (2nd edn, Human Kinetics, 2004)

FURTHER EDUCATION SPORTING ACADEMIES
An opportunity for 16–18-year-old students to combine personal elite sport development with academic study at a local further education college. Sporting input is often from professional coaches focusing on physical and mental fitness, technical ability, tactical awareness, coaching skills and game play. There are possibilities in some institutions for accommodation with bursaries available to assist with fees. These developments, which began in the late 1990s, contrast strongly with the situation earlier in the decade when there was a decline in the amount of sport available in colleges caused in part by a lack of financial investment and a change in the terms and conditions of employment for lecturers. A move towards more academic courses also meant that practical sessions were replaced by theory. As a result of the need to attract more students some colleges began to introduce specialist sports academies, often in football and usually working in partnership with a local semi-professional club. Although successful in boosting numbers, the initial quality of some academies was questioned (Perlejewski, 2004). Some of the first coaches employed had a limited background in education; however, more recent appointments include specialists in conditioning, physiotherapy, performance analysis and diet. Previous critics have also highlighted a drive towards elitism at the expense of participation, although later initiatives have tried to provide more recreational opportunities (ibid.).

Another example of recent improvements includes the Programme for

Academic and Sporting Excellence (PASE). This is a full-time course of study which runs parallel to a minimum of six hours coaching per week and tends to focus on major team games such as football and rugby. Some programmes are now linked with professional clubs, whereby players are monitored closely for development with opportunities for regular guest coaching from club staff. NGBs have also shown interest in setting up their own sports-specific academies at some colleges. While it has been difficult for further education colleges to both access lottery funding and acquire sports college status (ibid.), there are opportunities to become a Centre of Vocational Excellence (CoVE). This award launched by the government-sponsored Learning and Skills Council in 2001 is in recognition of a commitment towards enhancing the employability of potential entrants to the labour market. By 2006, 400 further education colleges had been granted CoVE status.

See also: *Further Education Sport Coordinators (FESCOs)*

FURTHER READING

Perlejewski, A., 'Sports Academies Within Further Education', *British Journal of Physical Education*, 35 (1) (2004), pp. 19–20

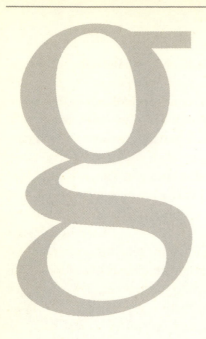

GIFTED AND TALENTED

The name given to an able children policy focusing on issues concerning identification and provision. Teachers are encouraged to identify five to ten per cent of each cohort and then provide enrichment programmes based on both curricular and extra-curricular opportunities. The term 'Gifted and Talented' was first used in 1999 as part of the government's 'Excellence in Cities' initiative (DfE) which was designed to raise educational standards in key urban areas.

Schools have often struggled with identification and provision within PE (Morley & Bailey, 2006). Ofsted reports initially suggested that implementation 'remains patchy' (2004, p. 15) with more recent accounts suggesting improvements in primary schools, although in secondary schools able students needed to be challenged more in lessons (Ofsted, 2009). Within the PE profession concerns centre on the need to identify potential and to recognise non-physical attributes (Morley & Bailey, 2006). There is also the fear of too much external interference from coaches and national governing bodies (NGBs).

It would appear that a large part of recent government interest in school sport has focused on identifying talent to promote national sporting success (DCMS, 2000) as part of the need to create a 'feel-good factor' for the nation. This external pressure has perhaps been reflected in the National Audit for Talent Development (2005 in Bailey et al., 2009) which has revealed that identification in schools has been overwhelmingly based on physical sporting success outside of lessons rather than on achievements in PE curriculum time. The same report also discovered that teachers found it difficult to identify based on potential and little recognition was given to non-physical abilities. Thus, Morley and Bailey's research (2006) suggested that PE teachers should identify the following abilities rather than just the physical: creative, social, cognitive and personal. Identification should primarily take place within lessons using a mixture of testing, observation and recommendations.

The most recent Ofsted report noted the impact of the Junior Athlete Education (JAE) programme (Ofsted, 2009). This form of provision is for Gifted and Talented students who will need help with lifestyle issues along with access to sports science assistance. It is most relevant to students who compete at international level and who may spend considerable amounts of time away from both their school and home environments. Although administered nationally by the Youth Sport Trust (YST) at local level, the lead should come from sports colleges. Teachers can train as mentors and arrange periodic meetings with students to advise and reflect. Williams (2008) suggests that JAE should form part of a two-tier model with the latter programme for the few pupils who compete at an elite level and, by comparison, a modified Gifted and Talented provision for other able pupils. Both programmes should involve teacher input as much as possible and be wary of too much external influence. Within lessons, Gifted and Talented has sharpened the focus on differentiation and encouraged teachers to acknowledge learning styles and pupil grouping. Here the writing of individual action plans (IAPs) could be a useful aid.

Gifted and Talented has often evolved to become a matter of personal philosophy rather than an externally driven initiative. It is imperative that it reflects the values that underpin PE while at the same time recognising the place of sport within this process. Teachers should remain at the forefront while still recognising the need to work with existing sporting frameworks.

FURTHER READING

Morley, D. & Bailey, R., *Meeting the Needs of Your Most Able Pupils: Physical Education and Sport* (David Fulton, 2006)

Williams, G., 'Gifted and Talented in PE . . . Or is it Sport?', *Physical Education Matters,* Autumn, 3 (3) (2008), pp. 19–22

GOVERNMENT

State interest in PE and school sport has evolved to the stage where various government departments have become major policy actors in determining its future. Many believe that government involvement has prioritised the interests of school sport above those of PE (Kay, 2003).

The Wolfenden Report (*see separate entry*) in 1960 signified the start of a real interest in youth sport and this has been a distinct area of public policy since the 1970s. The issues that surround government interest involve the desire for international sporting success, the need for social action and a response to pressure from the electorate for the building of state-funded facilities. In the 1990s it was the personal intervention of John Major that saw a 'watershed in PE discourse' (Kirk, 1992, p. 2). A government white paper entitled 'Sport: Raising the Game' (DNH, 1995) launched the National Junior Sport Programme and saw the promotion of games in the National Curriculum. Along with the introduction of the National Lottery in 1994 this document personified the Major administration's attempt to engage in nation-building using elite sport success. It perhaps also signified an attempt to entwine PE and sport together for that very same purpose (*see Sport: Raising the Game*). Indeed, Houlihan and Green (2006) maintain that since this document PE has lost focus within government policy. Under New Labour, school sport has had a major role to play in social policy as part of the 'third way' (Giddens, 1998), which attempts to combine old labour values of social democracy with the principles of market forces (*see Education Reform Act* and *Local Management of Schools*). The promotion of social inclusion and best value, i.e. allocating budgets based on economic efficiency, are good examples of this. Moreover, the continuing development of school sports colleges (SSCs) has personified Labour attempts to work towards partnerships between education and community with regeneration as a common theme.

New Labour sports policy is characterised by cross-departmental working within central government and an alliance with external bodies such as the YST – please see Table G.1: Government Responsibility for PESS for departmental responsibilities. This has been an interesting development given the scepticism that has surrounded previous collaboration across departments (Houlihan in King, 2009). The Department for Culture, Media and Sport (DCMS) replaced the Department for National Heritage (DNH) in 1997. Although it has responsibility for after school sport it has been suggested that it has limited impact and authority compared to other departments (Green, 2008). PE is the responsibility of the Department for Culture, Schools and Families (DCSF), which many believe has more political power, although PE is not a priority (ibid.). This separation undoubtedly presents a confusing picture and has helped to form the impression that the government view PE as physical activity that takes place within the curriculum while school sport is for activities outside of normal school time. Nevertheless, there can be little doubt that school sport has emerged as an area of considerable government interest, although its political distinction from PE created by the placement in a

Table G.1: Government Responsibility for Physical Education and School Sport (PESS)

Central Government Ministry	Department for Culture, Media and Sport (DCMS)	Department for Culture, Schools and Families (DCSF)	Department of Health
Main responsibilities related to PESS	Sport England, after school sport, National Lottery	PE in the National Curriculum, community use of sports facilities	Health promotion and education (physical activity focus)
Examples of national and regional government agencies and key partnerships	Sport England, UK Sport, regional sports bodies	Local authorities	Regional health authorities, primary care trusts
Examples of national non-government organisations	Central Council for Physical Recreation (CCPR), National Playing Fields Association (NPFA), governing bodies of sport	Youth Sport Trust (YST), voluntary sector school sport organisations, teaching unions, CCPR, NPFA	Various voluntary and community sector bodies

Source: adapted from King (2009: 70) based on Houlihan (1997: 97) Copyright Elsevier

g

separate department has limited the contribution of teachers from having any real influence (Houlihan in King, 2009).

It is the YST (*see Youth Sport Trust*) that has emerged as the most prominent government mouthpiece over the years. Supported by the school sports college (SSC) network, Ofsted and PESSYP it has met with little opposition from PE professionals and Sport England (Houlihan and Green, 2006; in King, 2009).

See also: *Policy*

FURTHER READING
King, N., *Sport Policy and Governance: Local Perspectives* (Elsevier, 2009)

GROWTH
The dominant biological activity for the first two decades of human life. Research into this topic looks at the increase in the size of the body as a whole and/or the size attained by specific parts of the body. The concept of growth is linked with *maturation* although definitions of the latter are essentially problematic: 'the process of becoming mature, or progress toward the mature state' (Malina et al., 2004, p. 4). Maturation can occur in all tissues, organs and organ systems, referring to the timing and tempo of progress towards the mature biological state. Rates of progress can vary and it is possible to have the same growth between subjects but for individuals to differ in terms of development towards maturity. In fact, it is this factor which perhaps best summarises the difference between the two concepts: growth focuses on size attained at any one given point in time, while maturation concerns the rate in attaining adult size and maturity.

Research into both growth and maturation involves the measurement and observation of cellular processes. Factors that influence the development of both concepts include:

- Heredity
- Hormones
- Nutrients
- Environmental considerations

Although research concerning these factors is prolific, less information is available on somatic (changes in body type), skeletal, sexual and dental maturation (ibid.). Of particular interest are the effects of socio-economic factors emphasising the role of living conditions, family size and ethnic origin in the development of children. With regard to sport, and especially for those children who engage at elite level, concern has been expressed over both the physiological and psychological effects of intense training. However, research has shown that these children grow in a similar manner to non-athletes and that any variation in body size is a consequence of the requirements in sport specific programmes (ibid.). While the effects of regular training do not affect growth in height, skeletal, sexual and somatic maturation, it can significantly affect body composition, performance and other physiological determinants. Secular trends suggest an increase in both height and weight levels over several generations in developed countries and to a lesser extent in less developed nations (ibid.). Furthermore, closely linked to these studies is the realisation that due to inactivity and poor diet, obesity levels are also on the increase; various physical activity programmes in schools have been created to combat this trend (*see Intervention and Health Promotion Strategies*). Young girls are also starting their menstrual cycle earlier and this may have an effect on participation in PE lessons. This problem could be alleviated by presenting pupils with opportunities to wear more appropriate kit.

FURTHER READING

Malina, R., Bouchard, C. & Bar-Or, O., *Growth, Maturation and Physical Activity* (2nd edn, Human Kinetics, 2004)

h

HEALTH-RELATED EXERCISE (HRE)
see Health-related Fitness (HRF)

HEALTH-RELATED FITNESS (HRF)
Health-related fitness is a term that was introduced in the 1980s to encompass those activities and concepts linking the awareness of health to physical activity and PE. It considered the promotion of lifelong physical activity with a view to promoting healthier lifestyles and thereby potentially reducing the occurrences of cardiovascular diseases and obesity. However, through the 1990s academics preferred the term health-related 'exercise' (HRE) as opposed to 'fitness' to attempt to change many schools' emphasis on the 'fitness' element as they embarked upon 'strenuous and intense physical activity in PE lessons in pursuit of high fitness scores' (Green, 2008, p. 101). The focus of HRF and more latterly HRE continues to be on the teaching of a lifelong promotion for health through exercise and activity. Being physically active produces long-term desired heath-enhancing outcomes such as reduction of body fat, therefore also reducing the potential for obesity, lowering of blood pressure and improved psychological well-being (Green, 2008). In this context, it is the 'health-related'

aspects of fitness that tend to be associated with health and well-being, hence such components as strength, stamina (cardio-respiratory fitness or endurance), suppleness (or flexibility) and body composition are explored and their potential to improve the general health and well-being of an individual (*see Fitness*).

The significant contribution that PE has to make towards health promotion has been acknowledged in successive national curricula, delivery of which reaches a large proportion of the nation's young people. In the revised NCPE for England (QCA, 2007) the 'Importance Statement' refers to pupils learning about 'the value of healthy lifestyles' and making 'informed choices about lifelong physical activity' (p. 189). This is reaffirmed in the provision of the 'Key Concepts' (1.4, 'Healthy Active Lifestyles') and the 'Key Process' (2.5, 'Making informed choices about healthy active lifestyles') and in the 'Range and Content' elements, 'exercising safely and effectively to improve health and well-being as in fitness and health activities' (QCA, 2007, pp. 191–194).

Teachers need to be creative in how they promote such concepts through the PE curriculum, which is quite often dominated by games at the expense of lifetime activities, more so for boys (Fairclough et al., 2002). Considerations of the vehicle for delivery, then, are important but ensuring the key messages that HRE has to offer are understood by the pupils is of equal importance. Harris (2000, p. 18) suggests that pupils need to be 'motivated to be active and they need to feel good about being active'. Programmes need to be well planned and structured with learning through enjoyment as the essence in order to foster the promotion of lifelong participation. Harris (2000) suggests that there are several principles that the HRE programme should embrace. Included in these is the need to promote the idea that exercise can be a 'positive/enjoyable' experience, that it is for all and all can be good at it, that there is an exercise that is suitable for everyone and that it can be for life. It is important that pupils experience success and make progress in developing confidence in their ability to take part in long-term activity.

HRE can be included in the PE curriculum by using a variety of strategies, including: permeation throughout the other activities; as a discrete (focused) unit of work itself; on a topic basis, possibly embracing a learning across the curriculum approach in a variety of subject areas; and as a combination of each of these methods. Whichever method is selected,

h

it is important that the activities have a 'carry-over value' into adult life (Fairclough et al., 2002).

See also: *Healthy Schools*

FURTHER READING
Fairclough, S., Stratton, G. & Baldwin, G., 'The Contribution of Secondary School Physical Education to Lifetime Physical Activity', *European Physical Education Review*, 8 (1) (2002), pp. 69–84

Harris, J., *Health-Related Exercise in the National Curriculum Key Stages 1 to 4* (Human Kinetics, 2000)

HEALTHY SCHOOLS
A multi-agency initiative promoted by the National Health Service (NHS) and Department for Culture, Schools and Families (DCSF) that aims to engage primary care trusts, local authorities and schools. The claim is that 99 per cent of all schools are involved with 75 per cent achieving national Healthy School status. To qualify for the award schools must achieve targets through the four core themes of personal, social and health education (PSHE), healthy eating, physical activity and emotional well-being. Healthy Schools is linked with the Every Child Matters agenda, whereby evidence from the former can be used for the five outcomes required for the latter (*see Every Child Matters*). Areas of the PE curriculum such as health-related exercise can also make a contribution towards this award (*see Health-related Fitness*).

The initiative was introduced in 1998 utilising New Labour themes of governance and partnerships between government departments. In 1999 a 'Healthy School Standard' was introduced, which focused on the provision of two hours a week NCPE, the promotion of extra-curricular activities and the start of attempts to liaise with health sector agencies such as primary care trusts. By the following year this emphasis on the relationship between sport and health had started to become established with programmes aimed at the education of teachers on the role of exercise and physical activity in particular. This was also the year when sports colleges were urged by the government to look at health as a means of urban regeneration. By 2001 concerns over child obesity had become prominent, adding to the perceived need for increased action on health in schools.

Ofsted (2009) reported how schools have successfully used the Healthy Schools initiative to make positive influences on the lifestyle choices of young people. However, the same report suggests that only 20 per cent of the schools inspected use cross-curricular links to reinforce health themes. Harris (in Bailey & Kirk, eds., 2009) suggests that PE has never really acknowledged or fully embraced its potential contribution towards public health. She believes that teachers are unaware of programmes that could be used in turn to reinforce PESS. Often PE can be too focused on fitness, sport and performance, while health emphasises activity levels and participation. In surveys it was found that health professionals often perceive PE teachers as coaches and instructors (Harris in Bailey & Kirk, eds., 2009). Green (2008) is wary of any expectations that PE can help improve the long-term health of the nation. The limited contact time and the increased demands on the curriculum would make this very difficult. A similar concern is voiced by Talbot (2008) who warns of competing arenas within PE, only one of which is health.

The desire to protect PE from too many external influences should not overshadow a need for the subject to make a significant contribution towards public health. Lifestyle options involve the combination of many interrelating factors, of which physical activity is but one choice. If PE teachers can make programmes enjoyable, less performance based and equip pupils to make more independent, informed judgements then maybe the subject can make a more positive input towards achieving public health goals.

FURTHER READING

Harris, J., 'Health-related Exercise and Physical Education' in Bailey, R. & Kirk, D., eds., *The Routledge Physical Education Reader* (Routledge, 2009), pp. 83–101

www.healthyschools.gov.uk

HEGEMONY

Taken from the writings of an Italian political theorist named Gramsci (1971), this sociological concept argues that the ideas of a dominant class in society are willingly accepted by subordinate groups. The process involved doesn't have to be coercive but based more on moral and ideological forces instead. Gramsci maintains that this is what holds societies together, based on an intellectual and moral leadership which can uphold the status quo. The practices supporting dominant groups almost become legitimate as they are internalised and reworked. A good example of this is the emphasis on subjecting the economy to the principle of market forces introduced in the 1980s as part of New Right ideology and which are now applied to most public services, particularly education.

Further examples can be taken from history. Hargreaves, in his seminal work of 1986, *Sport, Power and Culture,* is a keen proponent of hegemony, particularly as an alternative to functionalism (a positive emphasis on the view that society is organised by definitive hierarchical structures). He refers to athleticism and Rational Recreation (*see separate entries*) as an attempt made by the newly emerging middle classes to maintain power through the use of sport. This happened first by instilling values of loyalty, courage and fair play through the public school boys and then later through jobs in positions of responsibility acquired by the same. By promoting sport to those employees in their authority the bourgeois were transmitting similar values to the working classes, which Hargreaves states was necessary to maintain social order and control systems of power. However, although hegemony implies a ready acceptance from subordinate groups Hargreaves expounds the notion that struggles are involved by suggesting the working classes reacted differently according to both geographical location and the type of sport involved. Football, then, reworked itself through working-class culture with an adapted set of values, although bourgeois influence was never too far away – as shown by brewery sponsorship of the game. The values of athleticism, which also became known as 'the games ethic', by the early part of the 20th century became all-pervasive in state grammar schools to the extent that Mangan (cited in Kirk, 1992) sees this as a 'significant cultural hegemonic process at work' (p. 89). So, by copying the games-playing traditions of the public schools was this a bourgeois attempt at social advancement by adopting the pastimes of the upper classes who were also the law makers? A reconstructed games ethic based on public school athleticism also permeated throughout the 1960 Wolfenden Report (*see separate entry*) on youth sport. So, in attempting to promote sport as a panacea for juvenile delinquent behaviour, the report perhaps once more merely upheld existing hegemony (Hargreaves, 1986).

Critics of hegemony suggest that too much attention is afforded to extrinsic factors such as existing power structures rather than intrinsic considerations involving peoples feelings and personal relationships (Haywood in Mangan & Small, eds., 1986). However, to understand the influences on PE the concept does encourage the enquirer to ask questions and to look for deeper meanings. Thus, government, media, family and other cultural forms are important, particularly if they support the practices of a dominant class. Cultural hegemony itself can be difficult to break down but education could be a good starting point, especially if it promotes equality across social classes and encourages free thinking. However, many schools support existing systems of power through citizenship and hierarchies of management where top-down models still persist. For example, does strict adherence to school uniforms suggest over-conformity to existing societal practices and ideals? Gender issues within the curriculum can point towards a hegemonic masculinity which in PE manifests itself through segregation in lessons, attitudes towards dance and stereotypical images of how PE teachers should look – here, a dominant male, mesomorph body type is often portrayed. It is also possible to propose that a hegemonic curriculum exists – a term to describe PE programmes based on propositional knowledge (the acquisition of facts and skills rather than understanding) driven by pedagogy and assessment (*see separate entries*). This would suggest that teachers are so used to delivering utilising styles designed to inculcate facts that other more child-centred forms of teaching are forgotten about.

There is even a view that such a hegemonic approach is designed to protect the power of the dominant classes in society by not encouraging children to reason and to critically analyse (Fitzclarence & Tinning in Kirk & Tinning, eds., 1990).

FURTHER READING

Hargreaves, J., *Sport, Power and Culture: A Social and Historical Analysis of Popular Sports in Britain* (Polity Press, 1986)

HIGH QUALITY PHYSICAL EDUCATION

The term 'high quality' in connection with PESS has been used increasingly in policy documents and discussion in recent years. In October 2002, the PESSCL strategy was launched by the government, the key objective of which was to deliver the government's Public Service Agreement target (*see separate entry*), aimed at increasing the percentage of school children who take part in high quality PESS both within and beyond the curriculum. PESSYP, launched in January 2008, continued the government's commitment to improve the quantity and quality of PE and sport undertaken by young people aged 5–19 in England. Central to this is the issue of what (high) quality PE actually consists of. Kay (1998) suggested that fundamental to this question is also the consideration of why PE is important, what is provided and how it is delivered. Talbot (2007), argues that there are two key areas, first the process of learning and teaching and second, inclusion – meeting the needs of all pupils. As a starting point to providing high quality PE, a broad and balanced experience for all pupils and its effective implementation is also important. Planning the effective use of teaching time, available space and resources, the continuous monitoring of progress and the rewarding and celebrating of pupil achievements all have their role to play. Teachers delivering high quality PE have shared high expectations of their pupils, build on prior learning effectively, provide stimulating learning experiences and involve pupils in a variety of roles. They also inspire and motivate pupils by being committed, enthusiastic teachers who value the contributions of their pupils. The booklet 'Learning Through PE and School Sport' (DfES/DCMS, 2003) first outlined the meaning of what high quality PE and school sport comprised. It introduced the ten 'pupil outcomes', an indicator of what should be seen in young people who experience high quality PESS. These were then elaborated upon in 'High Quality PE and Sport for Young People' (DfES/DCMS, 2004) which sets out a framework for high quality PE teaching. Then, *Do you have High Quality PE and Sport in your School?* (DfES/DCMS, 2005) allowed leaders and teachers to use the outcomes to carry out self-evaluations on the quality of PESS in their schools and to use the findings to put together plans to improve provision. The ten outcomes of high quality suggest that pupils who experience this are: (summarised)

1   Committed to PE and sport and see it as a central part of their lives – both in and out of school.
2   Know and understand what they are trying to achieve and how to go about doing it.
3   Understand that PE and sport are an important part of a healthy, active lifestyle.
4   Have the confidence to get involved in PE and sport.

5   Have the skills and control that they need to take part in PE and sport.

6   Willingly take part in a range of competitive, creative and challenge-type activities both as individuals and as part of a team or group.

7   Think about what they are doing and make appropriate decisions for themselves.

8   Show a desire to improve and achieve in relation to their own abilities.

9   Have the stamina, suppleness and strength to keep going.

10 Enjoy PE, school and community sport.

FURTHER READING

Department for Education and Skills (DfES)/Department for Culture, Media and Sport (DCMS), *Do You Have High Quality PE and Sport in Your School: A Guide to Self-evaluating and Improving the Quality of PE and School Sport* (DfES, 2005)

Department for Education and Skills (DfES)/Department for Culture, Media and Sport (DCMS), *High Quality PE and Sport for Young People: Guide to Recognising and Achieving High Quality PE and Sport in Schools and Clubs* (DfES, 2004)

Kay, W., 'Physical Education: A Quality Experience for All Pupils', *British Journal of Teaching Physical Education,* 37(1) (2006), pp. 26–30

Talbot, M., 'Quality', *Physical Education Matters,* 2 (2) (2007), pp. 6–8

i

IDEOLOGY

Often expressed merely as a collection of political and social ideas, there are many other interrelating forces within the understanding of this concept. Both Hargreaves (1982) and Althusser (1971) believe that governments transmit ideology most forcibly and predominantly through education. Althusser argues that teachers can do very little to resist and that they will always have to serve a dominant ideology that they are powerless to change. Given the plethora of educational initiatives faced by teachers in the last twenty years, then this surely has to be one of the biggest contemporary challenges for teachers. Social responsiveness is important but so is social critique; how will newly qualified teachers comply with future educational change? Can ITE provide an acceptable balance between the two responses?

Althusser (1971) suggests that government ideology as transmitted through education helps to maintain the working class in a subordinate position. This is very much an historical view based on the traditional under-achievement of lower socio-economic groups in education and subsequent lack of opportunity to progress in society. There are similarities here with hegemony (*see separate entry*), although Kirk (1992) sees some limitations as it refuses to recognise the existence within society of a number of different ideologies by choosing instead to concentrate on the one dominant message. Ideologies within PE are particularly interesting because those involved often have strong emotional ties based both on personal participation in PE and sport and on contemporary teaching experiences. Standpoints taken can include strong views on talent identification, health and sport performance. This can lead to competing groups that merely reinforce an ideological position based on personal experience, leading to rigid viewpoints. Penny and Evans (in Green, 2008) suggest that the discourses that surround these positions often reflect a government ideology which, by emphasising initiatives such as Gifted and Talented (*see separate entry*) that concentrate on the product rather than the process, has perpetuated the notion that content within lessons doesn't need to be altered. So, while initiatives within PE abound and policies to support them proliferate, has anything really changed within lessons themselves? It is this passive acceptance of change that informs government policy and can lead to the internalisation of such views by teachers who are then seen to be conforming with the prevailing occupational ideology. External checks then become unnecessary because the implementers share the aims of the policy makers. A good example of this is again the Gifted and Talented programme, which instantly resonated with those teachers who were consistent advocates of a PE philosophy based on providing for the needs of an elite. However, these views can be in direct contrast with those held by many other teachers (Williams, 2008).

Green's work (in Bailey & Kirk, eds., 2009) on the ideologies of PE teachers exemplifies this suggestion of teachers' complicity towards government policy. He revealed several differing philosophies, most of which deviated from academic definitions of PE. Moreover, personal standpoints were often confused, contradictory and lacking clarity; for example, when trying to explain how much emphasis to place on elite performance in an inclusive PE programme. Green uses the term 'justificatory ideologies' (p. 201) to describe teachers' defence of personal views and has attributed their evolution to a combination of personal sporting experiences and current teaching practices. Perhaps teachers need more encouragement to reflect; to examine personal philosophies particularly in the light of increased recent government interest in PESS.

FURTHER READING

Hargreaves, J., ed., *Sport, Culture and Ideology* (Routledge and Kegan Paul, 1982)

INCLUSION

This is a term often too easily associated with special educational needs (SEN) when it should refer to access within the curriculum for all regardless of ability, ethnicity or gender. However, as many of these other concepts, such as Gifted and Talented, appear elsewhere within these pages, this section will concentrate on SEN itself and related terminology.

The term 'special educational need' began as a reaction to previous, more discriminatory classifications that failed to acknowledge the many complex and differing needs of the individual. It gained impetus from the Warnock Report (DES, 1978) with subsequent endorsement from the 1988 Education Reform Act and the 1993 Education Act. However, there is a suggestion that SEN has become a discriminatory term in itself by presenting teachers with images of problems associated with access, achievement and ultimately segregation (Mittler in Macfadyen and Bailey, 2002). As a result, a call for 'inclusive education' has gathered pace, with the recognition that teachers need to fully include all pupils irrespective of their abilities.

The current provision for SEN pupils within PE presents a mixed picture. Green (2008) found that SEN pupils have both less curriculum time and less active learning time than their mainstream counterparts. Participation rates are also lower. Furthermore, SEN pupils do not experience the same breadth of activities and are far more likely to pursue individual activities rather than team games. Such findings have led Smith and Thomas (in Green & Hardman, eds., 2005) to suggest that PE teachers at present are working more towards integration rather than inclusion, which some teachers believe is more of an aspirational but ultimately unobtainable goal. Other concerns identified relate to a perceived lack of support for PE inclusion from both teaching assistants and SEN coordinators. Many PE teachers also feel that the challenges they face now have not been helped by a lack of training at ITE level, where the focus was felt to be more on concepts rather than on how to deal with practical teaching scenarios. In addition Smith and Thomas (ibid.) found that of the many classifications within SEN, the one that presents the greatest challenge for PE teachers is that of emotional and behavioural difficulties (EBD). However, those pupils with physical and sensory difficulties were viewed more favourably.

Green (2008) also believes that PE teachers are currently achieving integration rather than inclusion. The suggestion here is that teachers are unclear as to whether the desired goal for SEN provision is similarity, adaptability or even a different curriculum. However, Macfadyen and Bailey (2002) disagree with this observation of confusion, suggesting that this approach offers the teacher flexibility in a lesson. They endorse a five-stage approach proposed by Black and Haskins (1996) which is based on the assumption that each scenario will be different and that teachers should not be afraid to use as many different teaching methods as are deemed appropriate (see Table I.1). In many instances the approach to inclusion is merely another form of differentiation (*see separate entry*), particularly that concerning support. The use of teaching assistants to help with disabled children can be particularly useful, although time should be spent in effectively communicating requirements and expectations.

i

One of the root causes behind the uncertainty surrounding SEN in PE is a number of general policy goals that appear to contradict each other. Schools are encouraged to engage in active competition for more pupil admissions by presenting images of happy, physically able children, all of whom are perceived to be high achievers. This can conflict with other government calls to provide for those SEN pupils who hitherto would have been placed outside of mainstream education. It would appear that currently schools are happier to promote images of the former group of pupils in order to attract the extra resources to be seen as a successful institution (Fitzgerald in Bailey & Kirk, eds., 2009).

Such far-reaching issues for the provision of SEN pupils include the need to re-examine a teacher's philosophical approach to PE. Barton (in Macfadyen & Bailey, 2002) suggests that large parts of the PE curriculum are unavailable to SEN children as access is based on notions of 'normality' (p. 103). Fitzgerald (in Bailey & Kirk, eds., 2009) extends

Table I.1: The Inclusion Spectrum (based on Black and Haskins, 1996)

Mainstream activities	Modified activities	Parallel activities	Adapted activities	Separate activities
Total inclusion of all pupils	Differentiated rules, space, equipment, roles	Same game, ability grouping	All pupils play adapted game	Pupils play separately

this argument by proposing that PE has developed to focus on the ethos of those who can and those who can't. Consequently, this makes it difficult for teachers to work towards full inclusion in a learning environment that can sometimes place such an emphasis on the acquisition of motor skills. Furthermore, the same author (ibid.) calls for the PE profession to reconsider concepts of ability and disability; only then can true inclusion be achieved.

There is a real need for more research concerning SEN in PE. The abundance of policy statements have neglected the need to consult those who really matter within this whole process: the teachers and the pupils. If those professionals responsible for the welfare of all SEN children can concur on a truly inclusive approach then maybe progress within PE will become more evident.

FURTHER READING
Fitzgerald, H., 'Still Feeling Like a Spare Piece of Luggage? Embodied Experiences of (Dis)ability in Physical Education and School Sport' in Bailey, R. & Kirk, D., eds., *The Routledge Physical Education Reader* (Routledge, 2009), pp. 303–322

INFORMED CONSENT
In order for participants to make an informed decision about participating in research, it is ethically important that they are made aware of the nature of the study and what will be done with the data collected from them. According to Bell (2005), an agreement has to be reached between the investigator and the participants involved in interviews, questions and observations concerning how the data will be analysed and disseminated as it reduces legal liability on the part of the researcher. There are obviously concerns here with regards to covert observations, as the researcher may not want the subjects to know that they are being observed. This is important, especially if children or people with SEN are involved. They may need the additional consent of parents or schools to satisfy ethical requirements. The participants and/or legal guardians need to be made aware that they are free to withdraw their services or their data at any point within the research process.

The information given to participants about the research has to be comprehensible in order for answers to be given that are reliable and valid:

Researchers must take the steps necessary to ensure that all participants in the research understand the process in which they are to be engaged, including why their participation is necessary, how it will be used and how and to whom it will be reported.

(BERA, 2004, p. 6)

Generally, it is important that participants are aware of the nature of the research when being questioned if the researcher wants their answers to be informed. However, there may be times when the researcher feels it necessary for the participant not to have a knowledge of the research, particularly if by informing the participant the researcher feels that it will falsely affect the reliability and (or) validity of the responses. If there is the potential for bias being present in the answers through the researcher outlining too much information beforehand, then consent can be obtained at a later time, but definitely before the data is finally collated and analysed.

Cohen et al., (2007) identified four elements that should be taken into account when gaining informed consent from research participants:

1 **Competence:** where correct decisions are likely to be made when the participants are given the correct information.
2 **Voluntarism:** when the participants are aware that they can withdraw their support at any stage of the research.
3 **Full information:** something that the researcher can strive for, although it will be difficult if the researchers do not have all the information themselves.
4 **Comprehension:** making sure that the participants have an understanding of the nature of the research project, and if there are any potential risks in taking part, what they may be. This can often be done by providing a covering letter outlining what the research is about, what is expected from the participants, and what will be done with the data collected.

By taking these four features into account, the respondent's rights have been considered, which may ultimately absolve the investigator of any moral and ethical responsibility (Opie, 2004).

See also: *Ethics, Reliability/Validity, Research Methods (Data Collection)*

FURTHER READING

British Educational Research Association (BERA), *Revised Ethical Guidelines for Educational Research* (BERA, April 2004)

Cohen, L., Manion, L. & Morrison, K., *Research Methods in Education* (Routledge, 2007)

INTERVENTION AND HEALTH PROMOTION STRATEGIES

These are programmes instigated to increase physical activity both within organisations and within communities. They are promoted by multi-agency collaboration between health and education and can be either a national programme or a more localised initiative. Either way, change can be achieved through a combination of policies, laws and regulations.

Schools are often an appropriate setting for strategies as they target a crucial age group, involve all cohorts and already have health and PE programmes in place. However, government and political interest can hinder development due to the traditional stance taken on the privileging of games within the curriculum (Biddle & Mutrie, 2008) which has often weakened the lobby for health and fitness. Interventions in schools are often mainly at the primary age and can vary from initiatives targeting daily routines such as a walk to school campaign or action aimed at changing established curriculum content. A good example of the latter is the TOPS programme, which provided both free PE equipment and continuing professional development (CPD) for teachers. The research investigating the benefits of intervention programmes within PE has produced mixed results (ibid.). Here, attempts to increase exercise levels within lessons has undoubtedly improved pupils' physical fitness but conclusions are equivocal when looking at the lifestyle objective of improving the amount of physical activity taken part in outside school. Interestingly, where positive intervention has taken place it has tended to be through the tuition of a PE specialist, who may also be a primary teacher, and mainly in the later years of primary school.

Strategies designed to address inactivity, such as through school-based PSHE lessons aimed at improving lifestyle, have produced insufficient evidence (Kahn et al. in Biddle & Mutrie, 2008). Similarly, studies on the effectiveness of cycling/walking to school are inconclusive, although those children who do engage in this manner may be associated with greater levels of physical activity in teenage years (Biddle and Mutrie, 2008). Nevertheless, by investigating how children travel to school a start is being made on one obvious area within the exercise patterns of young people.

An example of a specific Intervention and Health Promotion Strategy is the SportsLinx project in Liverpool. Introduced in 1996 and based on a partnership between the local authority and higher education, SportsLinx aims to discover sporting talent alongside promoting lifestyle changes and setting personalised programmes for children. The project was unique at the time for being one of the first to take a thematic approach by researching children's involvement in sport, recreation and health through schools (King, 2009). Originally aimed at the KS 3 age group, it now targets the later years at primary school. The strategy starts with a battery of physical fitness tests conducted in school time and is followed by raising awareness concerning nutrition and opportunities for extra-curricular exercise. Data recorded is used to inform future policy statements; test results gained so far have revealed that Liverpool school children collectively achieve scores below the UK average (LCC, 2003). In 2003 this was considered to be such a cause for concern that a call was made for a children's exercise referral scheme. Data analysed within Liverpool from 1998 to 2005 has noted a decline in performance within both skill-related and health-related fitness tests for 9–11-year-olds (see Fitness). Even more worrying is the realisation that these results may be attributable to increases in obesity levels over the same period of time (LCC, 2009). The response to this data has been an increase in the number of opportunities available for children's physical activity both within schools and within communities. Although successful in terms of collecting data and raising awareness, SportsLinx is still financed through a combination of health and education sector funding rather than central government. It faces a constant struggle in terms of identity (discover talent or improve health?) alongside a lack of engagement within some schools (King, 2009).

Physical education itself is seen as an important context for developing health-related behaviours but perhaps cannot make any real changes to physical activity patterns or physical fitness levels (Biddle & Mutrie, 2008). Pressures on the school timetable may mean that this will always be the case. However, this could be different if PE teachers were able to effectively teach the importance of lifestyle change rather than emphasise physical fitness testing (see Health-related Fitness and Healthy Schools).

Intervention strategies can be used to complement existing health education programmes based on HRE and inclusive extra-curricular sports activities. However, concern has been expressed within the PE profession over competing arenas within the subject, with health vying alongside sport and education for a voice (Talbot, 2008).

Those responsible for the content of strategies should be aware that for programmes to be successful they should involve choice, self-improvement, personal mastery, enjoyment and be of moderate intensity (Biddle et al., eds., 2000). In addition, for schools they should be practical based rather than in a theoretical classroom setting, involving all age groups (Cale & Harris, 2006). Interventions should also complement NCPE requirements, target 'multiple health behaviours' (i.e. physical activity alongside diet, relaxation, stress management), and be of at least 12 weeks in duration.

FURTHER READING

Biddle, S. & Mutrie, N., *Psychology of Physical Activity* (2nd edn, Routledge, 2008)

Biddle, S., Fox, K. & Boutcher, S., eds., *Physical Activity and Psychological Well-Being* (Routledge, 2000)

Cale, L. & Harris, J., 'Interventions to Promote Young People's Physical Activity: Issues, Implications and Recommendation for Practice', *Health Education Journal*, 65 (4) (2006), pp. 320–337

j

JOINTS

The point at which two or more bones meet is known as a joint or articulation. When considering 'movement' in physical activity and sport, researchers are primarily concerned with the interaction of skeletal and muscular systems – muscles moving bones via tendon attachments. There are different categories of joint in the human body and they are classified according to their structure and the range of movement permissible in the type of joint. These classifications are:

- **Fibrous joints** (otherwise known as fixed, immovable or synarthroses – *'syn'* meaning together, *'arthro'* meaning joint). These allow no discernable movement and usually hold bones together with strong fibres such as in the structures of the bones of the cranium (the skull) which serve a protective function for the brain.
- **Cartilaginous joints** (otherwise known as slightly movable or amphiarthroses – *'amphi'* meaning on both sides). They are characterised by a tough, fibrous pad of fibro-cartilage positioned between the bones of the articulation. These perform an important shock-absorption and stabilising role, while allowing small amounts of noticeable movement, e.g. joints between the lumbar vertebrae.

● **Synovial joints** (otherwise known as freely movable or diarthroses –
  'dia' meaning through or apart). These are the joints most concerned
  with physical activity and sport as they allow the greatest range of
  movement. There are six categories of synovial joint but all have
  common features, including a capsule of fibrous cartilage enclosing
  a cavity containing a special lubricant called synovial fluid. This is
  secreted by a synovial membrane that lines the cavity. On the ends
  of the articulating bones can be found articular or 'hyaline' cartilage,
  which has a smooth but resilient quality and allows the surface of the
  bones to move freely over each other. Joint stability is provided by
  the strength of the surrounding muscles and supporting ligaments.
  Some joints have additional 'bursae' or sacs of fluid to reduce fric-
  tion. Joint stability is also assisted by strategically positioned pads
  of fat.

The categories of synovial joint are as follows:

1 **Ball and socket** joints, where the rounded end of one bone fits
  into a socket or concave cavity of another bone, thereby permitting
  movement in all three planes/axes, more so than any other synovial joint. Examples of ball and socket joint include the hip and
  shoulder.

2 **Hinge** joints, where the convex surface of one bone articulates with
  the concave surface of another so that the only permissible movements
  are flexion and extension.

3 **Condyloid** joints consist of an oval-shaped bone structure situated in
  an elliptical-shaped cavity. The wrist is an example.

4 **Gliding** joints consist of surfaces of two or more bones that only allow
  a gliding movement over each other, for example the metatarsal bones
  in the foot.

5 **Pivot** joints, where a bony process or 'peg' of one bone fits into the
  hole (or foramen) formed in the other bone, allowing rotation to occur.
  The joint between cervical vertebrae one and two (atlas and axis) is an
  example of this type of joint.

6 **Saddle** joints involve an articulation between a concave surface of one
  bone and a convex surface of another in a biaxial formation (movement
  in two planes without rotation). The carpo metacarpal joint of the
  thumb is such a joint.

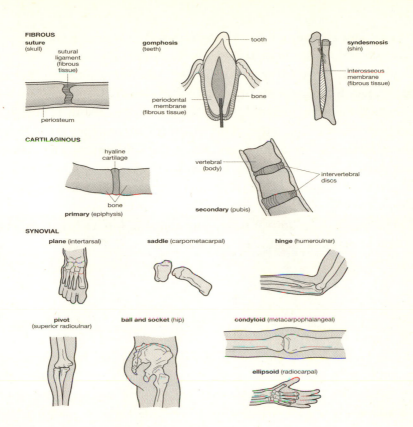

Figure J.1: Types of joint

The variety of movements permitted by the musculoskeletal system, via the joints, consists of:

- **Flexion:** where the joint angle decreases, e.g. 'bending' the elbow during a dumb-bell bicep curl.
- **Extension:** where the joint angle increases, e.g. 'straightening' of the elbow in the lowering phase of a bicep curl.
- **Abduction:** movement away from the midline of the body, e.g. raising the arm as in discus throwing.
- **Adduction:** movement towards the midline of the body, e.g. cross-over of the leg in javelin throwing.
- **Circumduction:** a combination of flexion, extension, adduction and abduction, e.g. arm circling.
- **Rotation:** a turning about the axis of the bone. It can be medial (inward) rotation or lateral (outward) rotation.

- **Pronation:** inward rotation of the radio ulnar joint so that the palm faces downwards as in dribbling a basketball.
- **Supination:** outward rotation of the radio ulnar joint so that the palm faces upwards as in throwing a ball upwards.
- **Plantarflexion:** at the ankle joint, pointing the toes downwards as in gymnastics.
- **Dorsiflexion:** at the ankle joint, raising the foot towards the tibia, e.g. stopping a ball with the inside of the foot.

FURTHER READING

Kirk, D., Cooke, C., Flintoff, A. & McKenna, J., *Key Concepts in Sport and Exercise Sciences* (Sage, 2008)

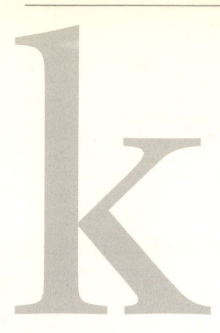

KEY SKILLS

These are the generic skills that students should develop at school and university, enabling them to be utilised effectively in both employment and life in general. These skills will also allow students to become effective learners while at university as they are essential tools for personal development and therefore higher attainment.

In 1997, the Dearing Report into Higher Education emphasised the importance of these skills and outlined four key areas:

1 Communication
2 Numeracy
3 ICT
4 Learning how to learn

Through PE, it is clear how these key skills can be interpreted in both an academic and a professional context. In the area of communication, students are expected to develop a range of oral, aural and written skills as part of their university course, through presentations, assignments and engagement in discussion, in addition to practical teaching episodes. Once in schools, effective communications skills are essential in the everyday teaching process; communicating with pupils, parents and colleagues as highlighted in the professional attributes of the qualified teacher status (QTS) standards (TDA, 2007). In terms of numeracy, course content may require statistical analysis, use of graphs to represent data, measurement and timing skills. As a teacher class percentages and improvement data will need to be analysed, and information recorded for examination entries, while timing and measurement of pupils' performances will be necessary within certain sports. The skills developed in using ICT, such as use of the internet, web-based learning, digital filming and analysis, word-processing and presentation and resource creation, will all have transferable value within the teaching context. These will be manifested in the development of resources, in the teaching context itself (digital cameras and laptops) and in the administrative role of the teacher in developing spreadsheets, for example. With PE being a valuable tool for delivering learning across the curriculum, these skills will be of great benefit in developing in turn those of the pupils. The importance of these key skills from a professional perspective is acknowledged in the QTS standards also. Standard Q16 in the 'Professional Knowledge and Understanding' section states that those recommended for QTS should 'know how to use skills in literacy, numeracy and ICT to support their teaching and wider professional activities' (TDA, 2007, p. 9). It is also recognised by the fact that to obtain QTS, professional skills tests in the same three areas must be passed.

The Higher Education Academy (HEA) has also produced 'student employability profiles' (HEA, 2007) that identify which skills should be developed through studying a particular subject. These skills have been mapped against skills 'employers observed in individuals who can transform organisations and add value early in their careers' (HEA, 2007, p. 4). Although PE comes under the 'sport' subject area in the document, it lists under 11 'transferable skills' that graduates should be able to 'plan and manage their own development and learning', and 'exercise communications and presentation skills, numeracy and ICT skills' (HEA, 2007, p. 132). To access the full document see 'Further Reading'.

FURTHER READING

Higher Education Academy (HEA), *Student Employability Profiles* (HEA, 2007), available to download at www.heacademy.ac.uk/resources

Training and Development Agency for Schools (TDA) at www.tda.gov.uk

1

LEADERSHIP AND VOLUNTEERING

Leadership and Volunteering is a stand-alone strand within PESSYP. The government have identified that children and young people have a variety of different career aspirations concerning involvement in the sporting community, and have recognised the personal qualities that children and young people gain from participating in leadership and volunteering programmes. The YST and Sport England work together on this strand within PESSYP, offering numerous programmes to children and young people. These include initiatives such as 'Step into Sport', 'Young Ambassadors' and the 'Young Officials Project'. Access to these programmes initially will be provided by the relevant School Sport Partnership (SSP), who will gain support and guidance from both the YST and Sport England.

Perhaps the most popular leadership award to date has been the Junior Sports Leader Award (JSLA), which stemmed from the Community Sports Leader Award (CSLA) launched by the Central Council for Physical Recreation (CCPR) in 1981. These were originally devised in response to growing demands from national governing bodies who wanted to see more volunteers in local clubs. In 1994 the JSLA was introduced as a similar course with a minimum enrolment age of 14. This is an award which fits in well with a school's KS 4 PE programme by giving pupils basic instruction on how to plan and lead physical activity sessions. A supervised assessment is then arranged, asking candidates to put this into practice by leading sessions with local primary school children.

Further recognition of increased impact came with a reference for the inclusion of leadership skills in both Curriculum 2000 resources and 'A Sporting Future for All' (2001). In 2003 all sports leader qualifications were assimilated into the National Qualifications Framework and in 2004 organisational responsibility was passed onto 'Sports Leaders UK'.

Tulley (2005) attributes the success of leadership programmes in schools to a number of factors. First and foremost is the claim that the content is enjoyable, practical and relevant, inculcating transferable skills for young people (Ofsted, 2009). The courses are popular with everyone, irrespective of academic ability. As a result around 100,000 sports leaders will be trained every year. Of particular interest to PESS has been the claim that JSLA has resulted in qualified youngsters being able to support PE teachers in extra-curricular programmes.

See also: *Physical Education and Sport Strategy for Young People (PESSYP), Sport England*

FURTHER READING
Tulley, R., 'The Growth of Sports Leadership', *British Journal Of Teaching PE*, 36 (4) (2005), pp. 25–26

LEARNING
A definitive meaning of this term is difficult to establish, as there are different interpretations linked to complex ontological and epistemological standpoints. Although learning can take place across a variety of circumstances, this particular definition deals with it in an educational setting. As a teacher, it is important to have a good understanding of the process of learning, as this aids the planning and development of strategies that will determine its effectiveness.

Kyriacou (2007) defines learning as a change in behaviour as a result of an educational experience. Childs (2007) adds to this by describing the change in behaviour as being relatively permanent and that it develops from past experiences. Pritchard (2009) also addresses a change in behaviour, but adds other aspects including a construction of understanding, and the acquisition or gaining of knowledge. Macdonald (in Wright et al., eds., 2004, p. 17) cuts straight to the point:

Shared by many perspectives on learning are assumptions that learning stems from experience, is a relatively permanent change, and provides a new potential to behave differently.

Kolb (1984) researched learning through experience. He argues that learning isn't outcome based, but a continuous cycle of holistic adaptation to the world. He identifies that the learner has an experience, reflects upon it, thinks about strategies based upon this, and then puts these into action. This has had an influence upon a variety of the theories behind learning styles that have become popular in schools over the last decade.

Despite many of the theories focusing learning around behaviour, it could be argued that this is placing restrictions on it; other aspects such as social skills, values and attitudes may also be learned. Behaviour perhaps has the most obvious links with PE as motor skills are more readily observable, and it is easier to see whether learning has taken place. However, if PE is more than just the ability to perform motor skills effectively then learning has to go beyond this.

Gagne (1975) identified five aspects to pupils' learning:

1 **Motor skills:** sequences of movements organised in simple and complex ways.
2 **Cognitive strategies:** problem solving and analysing.
3 **Intellectual skills:** reading, writing and mathematics.
4 **Verbal information:** communicating ideas, information and perceptions.
5 **Attitudes:** values and actions linked to beliefs.

These can also be applied to a more holistic definition of PE itself (*see Physical Education*) and demonstrate the different areas that contribute towards pupils' learning.

Marton (1975) looked at learning on a continuum moving from what he called 'surface learning' to 'deeper learning'. He saw surface learning as the rote reproduction of facts; as a basic assumption it could be argued that this knowledge was quantitative – the more that you know, the more you have learned. However, Spence (2001) reflects upon this by outlining that pupils are capable of passing tests, but are then unable to remember what it was that they had learned. For example, in PE teachers will often get their pupils to practise skills in a closed setting in the hope that these can then be replicated later in game situations. However, although mastery of basic skills may be essential to some aspects of a PE curriculum, a lack of knowledge of how to apply these skills in a more open environment may prevent pupils from understanding the nature of how to play within the activity. Therefore, developing understanding may be the key to 'deeper learning'. This is a movement away from a quantitative knowledge base, and focuses on seeking out meaning and transforming what pupils are learning by using their previous knowledge. Therefore, in a PE setting, pupils are taught how to make appropriate decisions during play, so that they have an understanding of how to use the skills they are learning. They are given information, which they use to find answers for relevant problems, both individually and in groups. By addressing issues such as team work, problem-solving and getting pupils to make decisions, physical education can allow pupils to deal with the social and emotional issues that they have to deal with outside of the class environment. This can often be a source of motivation for the pupils as it allows them greater ownership for their own learning, and provides meaning to other aspects of their lives (Azzarito & Ennis, 2003).

These two perspectives can be linked to behaviourist and constructivist (*see separate entries*) theories of learning. Meighan & Siraj-Blatchford (1997) looked at the role of learning and outlined three desired outcomes:

1 To be able to reproduce what the teacher knows.
2 To be able to synthesise from available sources.
3 To produce new insights or knowledge.

This has similarities with surface and deeper learning, and sees responsibility for the learning process transferring from the teacher to the pupil. Bloom's Taxonomy of Thinking highlights this in more detail (see Figure L.1). Learning that takes place at the higher ends of Bloom's Taxonomy will ensure that pupils are gaining understanding and making sense of what they are being taught.

See also: *Behaviourism, Constructivism, Pedagogy*

FURTHER READING
Pritchard, A., *Ways of Learning: Learning Theories and Learning Styles in the Classroom* (Routledge, 2009)

High level of cognition

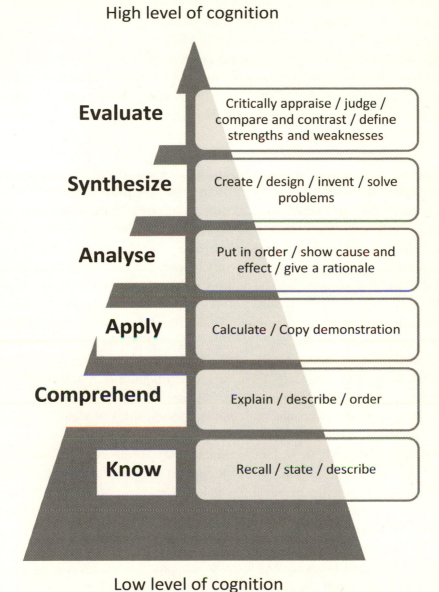

1

Evaluate — Critically appraise / judge / compare and contrast / define strengths and weaknesses

Synthesize — Create / design / invent / solve problems

Analyse — Put in order / show cause and effect / give a rationale

Apply — Calculate / Copy demonstration

Comprehend — Explain / describe / order

Know — Recall / state / describe

Low level of cognition

Figure L.1: Bloom's Taxonomy of Thinking

LEARNING STYLE

Developments and research into brain function have led to links being established with theories on how pupils learn in school. As a result there have been many new initiatives taking place in schools aiming to switch the focus from 'teacher-led' styles and strategies to 'pupil-centred learning'. The theory behind this is that teachers deliver to pupils' strengths and build upon their capacity to develop by understanding the range of ways in which people learn.

Researchers have produced a number of theories that suggest that people learn best in different ways, and that by teaching to their 'preferred learning style', the teacher is giving them the best opportunity to maximise their learning potential. This has come from research that demonstrates that humans are more or less receptive to different stimuli (Pritchard, 2009), and has even led to some of these theories being adopted and endorsed through government documentation (DfES, 2004).

There are estimates that the number of learning styles models in existence range from 20 to 120 (Sharp et al., 2008), and it is difficult to establish the ones that are of the most value, especially when some are very similar and allude to the same outcomes. The most established models include Visual, Auditory and Kinaesthetic (VAK) learning, and Gardner's Theory of Multiple Intelligences (MI); these are highlighted in the Key Stage 3 National Strategy document (DfES, 2004).

VAK is sometimes called the Perceptual Modalities Model, as it refers to the way in which learners prefer to receive data from the environment (Garnett, 2005). Pupils will be dominant in one or more of these modalities and, through research, Neuro-linguistic Programming has identified three particular styles in which pupils learn:

1 Visual learners learn better by seeing the teacher, as they interpret their body language, expressions and gestures. Pictures, diagrams and videos stimulate them, and they organise their thoughts by writing them down. As the visual modality creates mental images, they may use these by associating what they are learning with an image.

2 Pupils who learn best through listening are thought to represent the smallest group of learners (Tileston, 2004), and they are engaged by the speaker's changes in tone and tempo and by the volume of their voice. They need opportunities to discuss with others the content and concepts of the learning material.

3 Kinaesthetic learners learn best by doing (Pritchard, 2009). This links

to Kolb's theory of experiential learning, as learners need to actively explore the physical world (Garnett, 2005). Kinaesthetic learners do not learn best by having to sit and watch or listen as they may be easily distracted. They remember what they have done, as opposed to what they have heard or seen.

Fleming & Mills (1992) updated VAK to VARK to include Read/Write, although this is less widely cited. Howard Gardner, a Harvard professor, believed that each person is born with a full range of capacities and aptitudes, with some being stronger than others. His research outlined that all people are intelligent in different ways, and that IQ tests do not necessarily measure this. He identified seven initial intelligences:

1 **Bodily/kinaesthetic:** where people show an aptitude for doing things or for physical activity.
2 **Linguistic:** people were strong in aspects such as reading and writing.
3 **Logical/mathematical:** people who found it easier to apply logic to solutions and strategies.
4 **Visual/spatial:** where people can picture something in their head, but may find it more difficult to articulate in words.
5 **Interpersonal:** these people are more comfortable in groups and may have an outgoing personality.
6 **Intrapersonal:** people who are better at working by themselves.
7 **Musical:** where people use sounds, rhythms and patterns as a means of helping them learn.

An eighth intelligence proposed was *naturalistic*, which looked at a person's relationship with the environment, while *existential* and *moral* intelligences have also been recently considered. As they were 'uncovered' by Gardner at a later date, they were not included in the original list. People will have all of these intelligences, but some will be at a higher level than others.

These theories may well have implications for teachers and teaching as they allow pupils to learn in a way that they will find easiest, helping them achieve success in their learning. This may have links with intrinsic motivation. As a result, teachers can plan their lesson to incorporate a variety of teaching strategies that will cater for the particular learning styles of each of their pupils, leading to more pupil-centred lessons. It should be stated that Multiple Intelligence (MI) theories were adopted by educationalists, and that this was a move away from Gardner's original intentions as he felt that a regular intelligence test such as IQ failed to accurately measure what people were really good at.

Indeed, there are many concerns with the idea of teachers focusing solely on pupils' learning styles when planning. The fact that the National Strategy for Key Stage 3 includes both VAK and MI would indicate that these are endorsed by the DfES, and also that these are therefore more valid than others that are not mentioned. Those not mentioned include theories by Honey and Mumford, Myers and Briggs, and Kolb's experiential learning. This is despite the fact that these omitted learning styles appear to have been well researched.

A major issue for consideration is that the methods used to establish pupils' specific learning styles do not appear to be particularly valid or reliable. A questionnaire is the most established means of ascertaining a preferred learning style, and these question the learner about how they like to learn specific skills, find out information and solve particular problems. But there are lots of different questionnaires available, often for the same model, and asking different questions and requiring different answers. The formats of the questionnaires vary from multiple choice answers to rating perceptions on a scale. It is difficult to choose the one that is most applicable for each of the theories. Indeed, the National Strategy Document (2004) states that observing and talking to students is often as reliable as these questionnaires. This is expecting a lot from teachers, some of whom will undeniably have more knowledge and understanding of some of the particular learning styles theories being promoted than others. This may well be dependent upon the CPD training that a teacher has, or may be an area that they are personally interested in. Therefore, applying these theories to children's learning may be problematic. One concern is that people who have commercial interests in learning styles are the ones that are most vocal in the implementation of them within teaching and learning. These protagonists are brought into schools as part of teachers' CPD programmes, and are recommending that schools change their whole school teaching and learning strategies based around such models. The DVD that accompanies the National Strategy Document (2004) shows evidence of schools where the pupils wear labels, highlighting a preferred learning style, and this practice is in place throughout the curriculum.

The government outlined their own concerns by saying that research into learning styles is still highly variable with a very slender scientific evidence base (Hargreaves, 2005). There is even less empirical evidence from the classroom. If these strategies are being integrated into schools with little thought as to the validity and reliability of their implications, then pupils as a result may be being falsely labelled and taught through these modes.

Knowledge of these styles can be beneficial to the PE teacher simply in terms of making them think more about their pupils' learning, so that they change the styles and strategies that they use to make them more appropriate for particular activities. For example, the teacher might start the lesson with pictorial evidence of a skill or concept, explain it verbally, and then allow pupils to try it out for themselves. By categorising pupils as a specific type of learner it may be doing them a disservice, and putting a ceiling on their learning. Rather than serving as a motivating factor in that they are being taught through their own learning style, it could switch them off if it is found that a particular lesson wasn't incorporating such strategies.

There is also the notion that rather than making learning easier for the pupils, they need to be taken out of their comfort zones as this will be more beneficial in challenging them to reach the next level of learning.

See also: *Learning*

FURTHER READING

Department for Education and Skills (DfES), *Pedagogy and Practice: Teaching and Learning in Secondary Schools* (DfES Publications, 2004)

Pritchard, A., *Ways of Learning: Learning Theories and Learning Styles in the Classroom* (Routledge, 2009)

Sharp, J., Bowker, R. & Byrne, J., 'VAK or VAK-uous? Towards the Trivialisation of Learning and the Death of Scholarship', *Research Papers in Education*, no. 3, September 2008

LOCAL MANAGEMENT OF SCHOOLS (LMS)

The term given to the decentralisation of school budgets as part of the 1988 Education Reform Act. Prior to this, finance was administered mainly through education authorities as part of the tradition of devolving some government power at a localised level. Under the new arrangements schools were given almost total control of their own budgets instead of appealing to a local authority for help. The implications for the teaching of PE were to be far reaching.

The Conservative government in the 1980s had grown tired of working with local governments, which they saw as inefficient strongholds of left wing radicalism. By instructing local authorities (LAs) to pass on budgets in full, and in the case of Grant Maintained Status Schools missing councils out altogether, the government hoped to gain even more control over schools. Competition was introduced through the concept of formula funding. This involved market forces at two levels: first, by allocating finance according to how many pupils were enrolled and, second, within schools basing subject budgets on how many periods were on the timetable. This had an immediate effect on PE, which under the new National Curriculum had seen its lesson allocation reduced, especially at KS 4. The effects of formula funding were felt most acutely in terms of facilities – PE is traditionally an expensive subject for this very reason. Those who received less money under LMS, often due to falling rolls, and who were a local centre for other schools to use their swimming pools and playing fields, soon found maintenance to be a problem. They had previously relied on LA support to lend out these facilities for free as part of a goodwill gesture but now found upkeep to be a problem if they were experiencing less pupil admissions. In fact, swimming in PE lessons went into decline at this time with concerns over the cost of travel and pool hire.

In order to generate extra income many schools looked to encourage community use of existing sports facilities. This had implications for extra-curricular time allocation and the lending out (and collecting in) of equipment. Financial considerations were also paramount in the employment of new PE teachers, where often the cheapest option was sought in order to save money. Occasionally a PE teacher would not be replaced as some schools realised it was cheaper to hire a coach – many of whom were games specialists only. Other effects included the emergence of a crowded timetable where, for example, at year 9 a second foreign language took the place of PE for the benefit of more able pupils, who subsequently missed out on one PE lesson a week. At local authority level subject advisers were asked to re-evaluate their roles and in some instances a PE specialist was not replaced. Perhaps the most important consequence of LMS for PE was the realisation by many schools that PE/sport could be used as a 'marketing tool' to generate publicity and ultimately attract more pupils.

Senior management teams were quick to exploit this opportunity to the extent that in many cases sport became more important than PE (Penny & Evans, 1999). Teachers felt under pressure to produce winning school teams, often assuming the role of coaches instead.

Given that LMS was introduced at about the same time as the National Curriculum, any study of ERA would need to appreciate that the two are interlinked. The financial constraints placed upon PE as a result of this new legislation meant that NCPE never really developed in schools (Penny & Evans, 1999). Furthermore, the delegation of school budgets at all levels has meant that financial considerations have remained uppermost in the minds of PE teachers ever since.

See also: *Education Reform Act (ERA)*

FURTHER READING
Penny, D. & Evans, J., *Politics, Policy and Practice in PE* (Spon Press, 1999)

1

m

METHODOLOGY

It is necessary to distinguish between the methodology and the methods used to collect data for a research project. Although they are logically linked, they are often confused with each other (Grix, 2002). The initial aim of the methodology is to reflect upon the epistemological approach that will be used to shape a research project. Opie (2004) calls this philosophical thinking work, as it determines the beliefs or assumptions that guide the researcher in their research. A subsequent rationale for structuring a methodology is to construct a description and an analysis of the methods used to reveal limitations in the research, and to clarify potential consequences when adhering to the particular approaches (Wellington, 2000).

A methodological approach ties in with the researcher's ontological and epistemological standpoint, as it is these positions that shape the research. It determines the questions asked, how they are posed and how they are answered (Grix, 2002). The methodology follows a logical progression from the researcher's epistemology, which has in turn been shaped by their ontology. For the novice researcher, it is therefore appropriate to begin the process with a research question, rather than a specific method, as this may cause confusion if they were to use approaches that were incompatible with their ontological assumptions and epistemological position (positionality). An example may be an undergraduate seeking to determine pupils' feelings about the approach that their school takes on extra-curricular activities. The positionality of the researcher will affect how they proceed with uncovering knowledge of social behaviour, this being the research question that they wish to answer. In order to make sense of social reality (or to answer different questions about physical education), the researcher will follow either a positivist or an interpretivist paradigm. These opposite paradigms dictate different methods for collecting and analysing the data.

Positivism was until recently the most common form of research within physical education. The positivist uses an objective perspective when investigating the social world, and uses quantitative statistical methods to gather and collate the data (Curtner-Smith in Laker, ed., 2002). Their aim is to view the world from a position that is unbiased and detached:

With regard to ontology, positivism postulates that the social world external to individual cognition is a real world made up of hard tangible and relatively immutable facts that can be observed, measured and known for what they really are.

(Sparkes, 1992, p. 20)

Observations are key to collecting the data, although the issue of the researcher remaining objective, controlling the variables and replicating the same conditions are areas of potential difficulty when conducting the investigation.

In direct contrast to the positivist paradigm is the interpretivist approach. This can form a number of different qualitative methods, but for the novice researcher it is simpler to group them as one. The interpretivist researcher has a belief that the way in which positivists view the physical world cannot be applied to the social world (Sparkes, 2002). As human behaviour is based upon different beliefs and percep-tions that vary from person to person they have adopted a subjectivist or constructivist epistemology. An interpretivist researcher will be unable to see the world without their own place in it, and therefore there is the potential for multiple 'truths' as all data will have value attached. The interpretivist will often use multiple techniques to collect the data, generally selecting from interviews, questionnaires, focus groups and observations. By using two or more interpretations of the data, interpretivists believe that this will allow for richer information, and a broader view of social reality. To reach an answer to the research question, the data will be coded and categorised, highlighting relevant themes as evidence. The interpretivist researcher will acknowledge that bias will be present as part of the research process, but this will be recognised and highlighted during the methodology.

See also: *Epistemology/Ontology, Research Approach, Research Methods (Data Collection)*

FURTHER READING

Curtner-Smith, M., 'Methodological Issues in Research' in Laker, A., ed., *The Sociology of Sport and Physical Education* (Routledge, 2002), pp. 36–57

Sparkes, A., 'The Paradigms Debate: An Extended Review and a Celebration of Difference' in Sparkes, A., ed., *Research in Physical Education and Sport* (Falmer Press, 1992), pp. 9–60

MODEL COURSES

A syllabus or programme of physical activity emanating from the government in the early part of the 20th century. The intention was for schools to imitate and replicate these advisory documents. After the strong military influence behind the 1902 Model Course, subsequent guidelines became more child centred in their content and less didactic, with a greater emphasis on the use of imagination and creativity.

In 1904 the Board of Education moved away from working with the War Office for programmes of physical training and towards collaborating with the Medical Department. Although some military drill was retained in the new syllabus of that year, greater emphasis was placed on health and therapeutic aspects with a shift back towards Swedish drill (*see Drill*). The activities to be taught were presented in the form of tables to be followed. Teachers rather than army officers were once again in charge, although they had limited options regarding content. Play activities in the open air were encouraged with a stress on posture and circulation. The syllabus recognised for the first time the needs of different age groups and encouraged suitable clothing to be worn. By 1909 the chief medical officer, George Newman, had influenced the writing of a new syllabus with an even greater concentration on health and hygiene. Games and recreational activities like dancing and skipping had also started to become more prominent. Local authorities were told to make provision for the training of teachers in physical training.

After World War One Newman believed physical training in schools to be the most expedient method of improving children's health. More schools were built with gymnasia and playing fields; returning soldiers hoped for a fairer society. By the time of the 1919 Physical Training Syllabus for Schools, playgrounds had started to be marked out. The syllabus itself encouraged the use of small, sided games along with the introduction of dance steps and the existing tables of instruction were remodelled with more responsibility given back to the class teacher. The resulting interest from potential teachers led to the start of one-year training courses for women.

The Model Course of 1933 was introduced in the midst of growing poverty and depression within British society and physical training was seen by many as a positive distraction (Welshman, 1996). European influences within sport, such as Ling's Gymnastics (*see Expressive Movement*), and on young people in particular were now paramount and the 1933 syllabus is still held in high regard by many in the PE profession today. This is mainly for its detailed outline of lesson plans and also for breaking away from drill by introducing more creative and enjoyable activities. So, the development of skill was encouraged through elements of play and the emphasis on group work and partner work was seen as confirmation that a more child-centred form of teaching was now in the ascendant. Was this the birth of PE for the masses?

FURTHER READING

Board of Education, *Syllabus of Physical Training for School* (HMSO, 1933)

Welshman, J., 'Physical Education and the School Medical Service in England and Wales, 1907-1939', *The Society for the Social History of Medicine,* 9 (1996), pp. 31–48

MOTOR DEVELOPMENT

The process through which a child acquires movement patterns and skills (Malina et al., 2004). Factors involved include maturation, heredity, body size and body composition, and previous motor experiences. Environmental considerations are paramount, both physical and social.

Apart from those with specific physical disabilities, all children have the potential to acquire a repertoire of fundamental motor skills (*see Fundamental Movement Skills*). Moreover, movement patterns gained during infancy and early childhood can have an influence on later motor behaviours. Here, 'milestones' are used to signify the attainment of postural (such as balance), locomotor (for example walking, running) and prehensile (i.e. those actions involving the ability to grip or grasp) achievements. Between the ages of five and eight years, basic motor skills are well developed, although there are considerable differences between children. Progress is attained through practice and instruction leading to the acquisition of skill. Specific increases in performance have been found in speed-related activities at this age group, while improvements in throwing, jumping and strength are more gradual (ibid.).

Gender differences within motor development are prominent. The motor performances of girls in some tasks improve in a linear fashion from six years of age to about 14 years and then appear to plateau. Although previous research has pondered over the reasons why this should be the case (biological or social?) there is now the intriguing possibility that with increased sporting opportunities for adolescent girls this may change (ibid.). Meanwhile, it is at this stage that boys tend to show a marked improvement, particularly in strength-related activities. Generally, differences in performances during childhood and adolescence can be attributed to age, height, weight, physique and body composition. However, there are other factors involved and the interrelating roles of motivation, practice, learning and other cultural opportunities has yet to be fully investigated (ibid.).

FURTHER READING
Malina, R., Bouchard, C. & Bar-Or, O., *Growth, Maturation and Physical Activity* (2nd edn, Human Kinetics, 2004)

MUSCLE CONTRACTION
Muscles produce movements by contracting. Skeletal muscles exist in pairs known as antagonistic pairs, consisting of the agonist or prime mover, which effects a particular movement, and an antagonist, which produces

the opposite movement. The skeletal muscles consist of muscle fibres, the myofibrils of which have end to end contractile units known as sarcomeres. There are different types of muscle contraction:

- **Concentric and eccentric:** concentric contractions are the most commonly used in physical activity. The muscle shortens as it produces tension to overcome a resistance. This is known as positive work. The action of the bicep during the upward movement of a dumb-bell curl is an example. In an eccentric contraction, tension is produced as the muscle 'lengthens' (negative work) and the external resistance overcomes the working muscle. An example is the action of the bicep in the lowering movement of the bicep curl exercise.
- **Isometric:** the muscle remains the same length as it contracts and no movement is produced. The tension of the muscle is equal to the force of the resistance and the joint angle remains constant. An example of an isometric contraction is pushing against an immovable object, or holding a static position as in a handstand.

m

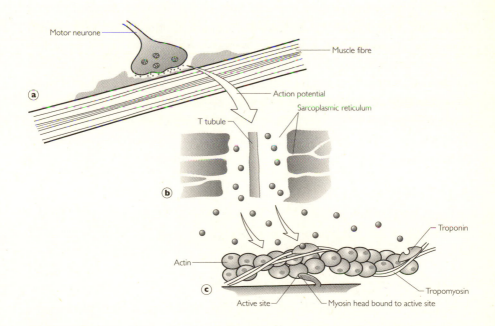

Figure M.1: A Sarcomere During Muscle Contraction and Relaxation

- **Isokinetic:** involve the constant speed of contraction over the range of movement. This type of contraction requires specialist equipment such as a hydraulic exercise machine.

The microscopic actions within the sarcomere of the muscle causing contractions are known as the 'sliding filament theory'. Actin and myosin micro-protein filaments within the sarcomere are stimulated by a nerve impulse causing depolarisation and the release of calcium ions from the sarcoplasmic reticulum. The calcium ions bind to the globular protein troponin, changing the shape of the troponin-myosin complex and causing the actin active sites to be exposed. The filaments ultimately slide over each other in a form of 'ratchet' mechanism through cross-bridge attachments, forming actomyosin. As the filaments slide past each other, the 'Z lines' of the sarcomere are drawn closer together (there is no change in the actual length of the filaments during this process). This is repeated in other sarcomeres along the length of the muscle and the muscle as a whole is seen to contract. Energy for the process is derived from ATP hydrolysis.

FURTHER READING

McArdle, W.D., Katch, F.I. & Katch, V.L., *Essentials of Exercise Physiology* (2nd edn, Lippincott Williams and Wilkins, 2000)

Wilmore, J.H. & Costill, D.L., *Physiology of Sport and Exercise* (Human Kinetics, 2004)

n

NATIONAL CURRICULUM

The very first National Curriculum for Physical Education (NCPE) became a statutory requirement for all state schools in 1992. Even after three subsequent changes (1995, 2000 and 2007) the design is still to establish an inclusive entitlement for all pupils to access a curriculum containing appropriate breadth and depth. NCPE is also designed to set a number of standards so that pupil performance can be measured and compared across a number of groups and settings. By doing so NCPE can promote continuity and coherence, enabling progressions in learning to take place particularly concerning transitions between the Key Stages. Through such a public statement as NCPE there are opportunities for various interest groups such as parents and employers to have full access to what is taught in schools. Awareness is then raised concerning curriculum content and how children are being prepared for both the workplace and the community at large.

School PE before the National Curriculum was often a matter of personal philosophy based on the availability of scant resources. Government-produced syllabi were advisory rather than statutory and standards were regulated by Her Majesty's Inspectors (HMIs) and some local education authorities (LEA) advisors. However, the Education Reform Act in 1988 (*see separate entry*) placed PE as a lower tier 'foundation' subject rather than the perceived to be more important 'core' and introduced the concept of compulsory assessment. Six areas of activity were identified – games, gymnastics, swimming, athletics, dance and outdoor and adventurous activities (OAA). NCPE stipulated that schools had to choose four areas at KS 3, with games as compulsory, and two activities from any area at KS 4. Following the recommendations of the Dearing Report in 1995 for a reduced National Curriculum, half units of work, involving less assessment requirements to be covered, were introduced to enable flexibility within and between schools. HRE (*see Health-related Fitness*) statements were also encouraged and games became compulsory at KS 4. Curriculum 2000 promoted cross-curricular elements including key skills, citizenship, numeracy, literacy and ICT. Knowledge, skills and understanding were promoted among teachers to inform planning and level descriptors stating specific requirements for attainment were formulated for assessment. Similar ideologies are found permeating throughout the 2007 NCPE, which asserted that young people should become successful learners, confident individuals and responsible citizens. The desire for extra breadth in the curriculum is reflected in the replacement of areas of activity with six themes ('Range and Content') which offer opportunities for pupils to engage more readily in non-traditional sports:

1 Outwitting opponents, for example in games.
2 Accurate replication, for example in gymnastics, swimming and dance.
3 Exploring and communicating ideas, for example in dance and gymnastics.
4 Performing at maximum levels, for example in athletics and swimming.
5 Identifying and solving problems, for example in OAA.
6 Exercising safely and effectively, for example in HRE.

Schools must offer at least four out of the six themes at KS 3 and at least two for KS 4. At primary level pupils must develop knowledge, skills and understanding through dance, gymnastics and games at KS 1 and select two more from swimming, athletics or OAA at KS 2.

Ofsted (2009) have found that most secondary schools meet the minimum NCPE statutory requirements at KS 3 and KS 4, although few institutions offer swimming and OAA probably due to problems of access to facilities and concern over the perceived risks involved (*see Risk Assessment/Management*). The same report found that the better PE departments used the four strands of Curriculum 2000 to assess pupil progress as opposed to using their own criteria. Green (2008) suggests that NCPE has encapsulated all the ideologies and discourses that have historically surrounded the subject with an emphasis on sport as a worthwhile cultural experience to meet these ends. Furthermore, he also believes that PE teachers have rationalised NCPE to fit their own personal philosophies. Such a statement supports those who wonder whether a National Curriculum really has made any difference to the pedagogical practices that surround PE (Penny & Evans, 1999). However, while the substance and content may not have changed too much for some teachers the presence of such a statutory requirement can put pressure on others to conform and comply. Ultimately, PE has had to come under the same scrutiny experienced by other subjects, a process that has probably contributed to its increased status within the curriculum.

FURTHER READING
www.curriculum.qca.org.uk

NATIONAL SCHOOL SPORT WEEK

n

As part of PESSYP all schools are encouraged to target one week at the end of June to promote sport based on Olympic values such as equality, excellence and friendship. Building on the gathering momentum for London 2012, activities should be cross-curricular in content. Participants are encouraged to take a 'sports pledge'; examples include promises to engage in more physical activity, to learn about a new country and to get involved in sports leadership. Teachers can request free resources to help with the week and ask for visits from Olympians and Paralympians. This initiative is controlled by the YST (*see separate entry*) and registration is available online. Specific examples of school responses seem to involve maintaining the traditional school sports day but with more of an Olympic theme such as the use of opening and closing ceremonies with the competing pastoral groups adopting names of specific countries. To develop leadership skills some secondary school pupils have organised a mini Olympics for invited primary schools. Other schools use the week to promote fun activities such as tug-of-war competitions. One school even planned to break the world record in 2009 for having the most number of people skipping for three minutes, an activity involving both staff and children. In 2008 the

National School Sport Week was used to promote intra-school competition by providing a resource pack based on collaboration between NGBs and SSPs. This development targets a middle band of children who hitherto have had a comparatively low involvement rate in extra-curricular activities. The aim is to achieve 25 per cent participation in total.

Critics of this initiative suggest that by focusing on just one week there may be a tendency to forget that school sport is a whole-year-round process, ignoring all the hard work that goes on often without the help of extra government resources (Wallis, 2008). There is also the concern for sustainability – can the interest initiated from such an event be followed up by further opportunities to engage? This will be the sort of challenge for which the PESSYP initiative (*see separate entry*) with its 'five-hour offer' of physical activity per child per week is designed to cater.

FURTHER READING

Wallis, G., 'National School Sport Week: Hitting More Targets But Still Missing the Point?', *Physical Education Matters,* Autumn, 3 (3) (2008), pp. 46–47

www.schoolsportweek.org

'NEW' PE

The collective term given for a group of child-centred teaching initiatives developed in the 1980s. The 'Great Debate' instigated by Prime Minister Callaghan in 1976 had raised awareness over a perceived decline in educational standards and with the call for a more centralised curriculum change was imminent. Public perceptions were tarnished by a teachers' strike action and a media interpretation that PE had eliminated competitive aspects from the subject. Consequently, PE teachers felt under threat from a number of different quarters and concern was expressed over the subject's survival.

The result was a number of innovations that were inclusive and child centred and perhaps ultimately clashed with the discourses and ideology surrounding NCPE. Thus gender issues were addressed by encouraging dance for boys and developing mixed lessons in appropriate sports. The teaching of games was categorised into invasion, striking and fielding, and net/wall – terminology useful when addressing breadth and depth for curriculum planning. Sporting festivals and cross-curricular themes were encouraged. Perhaps the most notable developments emerging at this time centred on the 'Teaching Games for Understanding Model' (Bunker and Thorpe, 1982) and health-related fitness (HRF). Both innovations had almost immediate impact and have become precursors for more contemporary developments in Sport Education and health-related exercise (HRE) respectively (*see separate entries*). Together they challenged traditional approaches towards PE by starting from the viewpoint that conventional practice had been based on an exclusivity which had privileged games for the elite in particular.

Critics of 'New' PE in the 1980s, mainly from the media, suggested that it was an expedient reaction to cutbacks in transport for schools and the selling-off of public playing fields. Some even suggested that HRF in particular was distracting teachers from their responsibilities towards games (TES in Kirk, 1992). In addition, with a backdrop of rising unemployment, attempts were also made to address the issue of changing leisure patterns by offering a wider variety of activities in PE that could lead to increased lifelong participation. However, by doing so the promotion of recreational activities such as tenpin bowling and horse riding over more traditional sports was also questioned. Generally, Kirk (1992) states that the true impact of 'New' PE was to prompt further discourse (*see separate entry*) surrounding the subject rather than to result in wholesale implementation.

FURTHER READING

Almond, L., *The Place of Physical Education in Schools* (Kogan Page, 1989)

Kirk, D., *Defining Physical Education: The Social Construction of a School Subject in Postwar Britain* (Falmer, 1992)

n

OSTERBERG, MADAME BERGMAN

One of the first pioneers responsible for the concepts behind PE and who epitomises the strong early female influence on the profession. Osterberg was a forerunner of systematic PE with her advocacy of Swedish gymnastics involving the use of wall bars, ropes, beams, horse and box. Her methods gained political support at government level (Smith, 1974). She had studied the scientific approach of Ling to gymnastics (*see Expressive Movement*) in Stockholm but came to London more concerned with the advancement of female emancipation.

In 1881 an enlightened School Board for London wished to improve levels of physical activity for young children and so appointed Osterberg to become a 'Lady Superintendent of PE'. While encouraging Swedish gym within this post she also opened in 1885 the first ever college for training lady teachers at Hampstead. Here, the Ling system for gymnastics based on the use of apparatus as a scientific approach to improve strength, flexibility and stamina was promoted. There were also elements of games, swimming and dance taught to predominantly middle-class ladies. In 1895 Osterberg gave up her original post to concentrate on the college, which had moved to Dartford. This then became the first residential PE teachers' specialist college.

Due to her strict disciplinary approach Osterberg was known as 'Napoleon' to her students. She was often guided by feminist motives as shown by her early replacement of male teachers with her own former students. She insisted upon high standards of dress and behaviour, for example her insistence on the wearing of gym tunics rather than the more fashionable corsets worn by women at the time. Her students soon became known as 'Madame's girls'. Dartford paved the way for the formation of other specialist ladies' PE colleges such as Chelsea (1898) and Bedford (1903). By 1915, when Osterberg died, there were some 1350 female practising gym teachers. There are some writers (for example McIntosh, 1968) who state that Osterberg's contribution has been overshadowed by other significant physical educationists such as George Newman with his drive to put health at the heart of school physical training syllabi (*see Model Courses*). However, her determination to establish continental methods of physical activity in England, and the training of middle-class female teachers in particular, cannot be understated.

FURTHER READING

McIntosh, P., *Physical Education in England since 1800* (Bell and Sons, 1968)

Smith, D.W., *Stretching Their Bodies* (David and Charles, 1974)

O

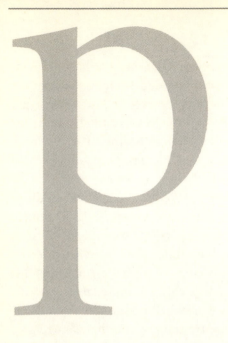

PANATHLON CHALLENGE

An interschool multi-sport competition established in 1996 with funding from commercial sponsors, government and charitable trusts. Schools from disadvantaged areas were targeted in an attempt to encourage sport by providing equipment, coaching and the chance to compete in an event organised regionally with progression to a national final involving badminton, table tennis, cycling, orienteering, athletics, basketball, chess, football and netball. Further support also came from Sport England who saw the selection criteria as matching one of their key target areas. Originally aimed at mainstream schools a disability competition soon followed and for a while both events ran in tandem each year. However, since 2005 because of increased government funding for mainstream school sport in particular, the Panathlon Challenge has catered solely for disability sport. As a result a diverse range of adapted sports is deliberately chosen to encourage participation and develop pupil self-esteem; approximately 25,000 children take part every year.

Organisers claim that participation improves pupil behaviour both within the sporting context and in the classroom (Hymers, 2004). A fair play charter is signed by all. Some schools use the Panathlon Challenge within their SSP and encourage feeder primary schools to engage ready for KS 2/KS 3 transition. The development of individual and collective excellence has also been claimed as a result of this competition, with some schools citing school team achievements and the progression of pupils into professional sport as evidence.

FURTHER READING

Hymers, J., 'The One and Only Panathlon Challenge', *The British Journal of Teaching Physical Education*, Winter, 35 (4) (2004), pp. 25–27

www.panathlon.com

PARENTAL CONSENT

Written parental consent is needed in advance for many aspects of PESS where activity beyond the regular daily planned curriculum takes place. This would include activities such as school clubs, team fixtures/practices, etc. Consent is also required for school visits, transport considerations and the use of video and digital images in PE. It is important to understand local authority and school requirements with regards to parental consent, and the necessary forms that need to be completed. Some schools request parental permission on an annual basis for a range of activities and permission to record and use images of pupils; for example, in displays of their practical work. It is prudent, however, to have parents/carers sign an informed consent form prior to any activity where images may be recorded, confirming the uses to which they will be put. An example Digital Imagery Consent Form can be found in *Safe Practice in Physical Education and School Sport* (AfPE, 2008).

It is good practice to liaise with the school educational visits coordinator to ensure that the activities undertaken in PESS requiring parental permission follow the same guidance as other areas of the curriculum, so that clear routines are established that are readily understood by pupils, parents and staff. It is also important for activities beyond the curriculum to have the head teacher's permission.

It must be pointed out that parental consent forms are only a participation 'agreement' between the parents and the school and teachers are still accountable in terms of their responsibilities. AfPE (2008, p. 17) suggest that consent forms are 'a signed statement indicating that the parent/carer has been informed of and understands the risks involved in an activity and agrees to comply with the conditions stated'.

Information that the parents/carers might require, particularly for trips and visits, includes:

- The date of the activity
- The time of departure and return
- The venue/location with contact details where appropriate
- The means of transport
- The objectives of the trip/visit and the range/variety of activities to be undertaken
- The names of the party leader/lead teacher and other supervising staff
- Any costs/voluntary contributions required for the visit (and information about payment methods)
- Expectations for pupil behaviour and participation
- Any clothing, kit, equipment required
- Insurance cover that is included

Schools in turn will require information from the parents or carers in addition to a signature of permission. The extent of required information will depend on the nature of the activity being undertaken and the duration; for example, visits involving an overnight stay or travelling abroad. Details might include the full name, address and date of birth of the student, along with contact details of the parent/carer. Also, any medical information about the student is essential, with dietary needs a consideration as well. Teachers should also consider whether it is prudent to contact students by mobile phone, text or email or via any internet source. Where this is undertaken for the purposes of contacting students with school-related information, the consent of both the head teacher and the parents should be sought.

FURTHER READING

Association for Physical Education (AfPE), *Safe Practice in Physical Education and School Sport* (Coachwise, 2008)

Department for Education and Employment (DfEE), *Health and Safety for Pupils on Educational Visits* (DfEE Publications, 1998)

PARTNERSHIP DEVELOPMENT MANAGER (PDM)

The role of partnership development manager (PDM) is a full-time position, and PDMs can be seen as the main driving force within the infrastructure of School Sport Partnerships (SSPs). They do not necessarily have to be qualified teachers and are based within a sports college, being the hub site for the SSP. They are responsible for the management of the SSP and in particular the line management of the school sports coordinators (SSCOs) and primary link teachers (PLTs). Their brief is implementing, overseeing and evaluating effective strategies to raise the provision of high quality physical education and school sport within the partnership. PDMs are usually experienced teachers, some of whom have previously had a management role within schools. The Loughborough Partnership (2009) found that 56 per cent of all appointments were female and that the number of PDMs holding qualified teacher status (QTS) was in decline (down from 93 per cent in 2004 to 66 per cent in 2008).

The emphasis on the term 'partnership' reflects the New Labour ideal of multi-agency collaboration, particularly in the desire to regenerate communities. The PDM is pivotal in helping the sports college to engage in community involvement through collaborations with the health sector and individual sports clubs. The Loughborough Partnership (2009) found that the majority of PDMs state that their SSP is meeting existing demand. Interestingly, with regard to the issue of tackling obesity as a clear, key objective, and remembering government concern for the topic, only 58 per cent of PDMs believe this is being addressed in secondary schools, while for primary schools the figure is 61 per cent. Whether schools will be directed towards clearer and more insistent directives on this topic remains to be seen.

See also: *Primary Link Teachers (PLTs)*

FURTHER READING
www.youthsporttrust.org

PEDAGOGY

Pedagogy is a term that is difficult to define succinctly and with clarity. English-speaking countries have tended to focus upon teaching, while other European nations have traditionally extended this to include

127

learning, and other related factors. Loughran (2006, p. 2) calls pedagogy the 'art and science of educating children' and highlights that this relationship between teaching and learning is what contributes to the development of knowledge and understanding.

As assumptions about the concepts of teaching, learning, science and art can vary widely, it is necessary to identify how they can contribute to the formulation of a definition. Hellison & Templin (1991, p. 151) stated that 'teaching involves artistry, qualities that defy precise measurement', suggesting that good teachers of PE will know intuitively what to do, and how to apply their knowledge appropriately and effectively in realistic settings.

Personal qualities such as intuition and reflexion (self-reflection) are tools that an effective PE teacher utilises to ensure that pupil learning is taking place. The beliefs that teachers of physical education hold tend to be based upon what their conception of PE is, and Green (2008) links this to areas of experience. If personality and experience are the keys to teaching PE effectively, it may be the case that spending a great deal of time developing theoretical knowledge should become less of a priority in ITE. This therefore highlights the importance of the scientific aspect of pedagogy, as it suggests that the development of teaching skills can be broken down into a series of tasks that can be mastered. The application of how different social variables can be identified and gained, and how this as a social science can be used to develop an understanding of teaching and learning, is key. Through this understanding, opportunities to reflect will aid the development of teaching skills. However, there may be a problem here, in that by becoming an expert through applied social science, the teacher may have the knowledge to develop effective pupil learning, but will lack the artistic tools to put it in place.

Watkins & Mortimore (in Mortimore, ed., 1999, p. 3) defined pedagogy as '. . . any conscious activity by one person designed to enhance learning in another'. They viewed pedagogy not as an art or a science, but as a craft. This description lends itself to something greater than a simple transmission of knowledge. Therefore, the managerial and organisational aspects of teaching and learning should also be included. The teacher's teaching philosophy, their planning and the styles that they use for instruction must be considered along with the pupils' preferred learning styles, the objectives of the lesson and the lesson content itself. Pupil monitoring, assessment strategies and the resources used to facilitate the learning could also be included under this definition. Thus, pedagogy can be seen as everything that the teacher needs to take into account within attempts to meet the needs of the learner in achieving the learning outcomes.

As pedagogy takes place across all areas of PE, it is crucial that teachers are aware of its importance. If it is the case that contributing pedagogical factors are developed with teaching experience, then this will indicate that there are differences between novice and experienced teachers. As pedagogy therefore focuses upon not just 'what' is taught, but 'how' it is taught, then teachers will need to consider learning when aspiring to meet the needs of their pupils. In addition to prior knowledge of their pupils, they will need to understand how learning takes place as '. . . all teaching methodologies have their roots in particular learning theories' (Rink, 2001, p. 112). This allows teachers to understand 'why' they teach in a particular way, aiding their reflexivity, and helping contribute to the development of a teaching philosophy.

For the PE teacher, knowing the most appropriate strategy of instruction to use at a particular time will impact favourably upon pupil learning. The two most common epistemological theories of how knowledge is formed are called behaviourist and constructivist (*see separate entries*). These give the teacher an understanding of how pupils learn, and this in turn allows them to think about the teaching styles that they can utilise. Linked to behaviourist modes of learning are the more traditional didactic types of teaching. Thus, direct styles of instruction are often observable in skill-based lessons, which tend to be teacher focused – particularly where a product or performance outcome is based upon a particular skill within a sporting activity. As a result, the emphasis is placed upon the development of the activity where it is often easier for teachers to observe when pupil learning has taken place.

A constructivist theory of learning focuses upon children learning from their experiences and from interaction with others. When the concepts behind PE have begun to move away from a performance- and skill-based ethos to a more child-centred and holistic curriculum, more emphasis has been placed upon developing the social, affective and cognitive aspects of the learner. There has been a perceived shift towards teaching the child through the activity rather than teaching the child the activity itself (Kay, 2004), although it would be interesting to establish whether this was indeed the case in practice. This type of learning allows teachers to use more indirect styles of teaching, and gives pupils greater opportunities to construct their own knowledge and understanding of

P

activities utilising cognitive function and social experiences. Therefore, the activity that the pupils are undertaking becomes a vehicle for greater holistic development, as the pupils are actively encouraged to construct learning for themselves.

Teacher's pedagogical knowledge will develop through their day-to-day experiences in schools, but by understanding the theories they will be able to consider the impact upon their planning, teaching and evaluating, and offer a rationale or justification for what they have done, or plan to do.

See also: *Epistemology/Ontology, Learning, Teaching Strategy*

FURTHER READING
Loughran, J., *Developing a Pedagogy of Teacher Education: Understanding Teaching and Learning About Teaching* (Routledge, 2006)

Mortimore, P., ed., *Understanding Pedagogy and its Impact on Learning* (Sage, 1999)

Rink, J.E., 'Investigating the Assumptions of Pedagogy', *Journal of Teaching in Physical Education*, 20 (2) (2001), pp. 112–128

PERSONAL DEVELOPMENT PLANNING (PDP)
This term has evolved over a number of years from various strategies designed to encourage students to reflect upon and evaluate their own learning. Another aim is to take ownership and responsibility for planning personal and professional development (Irons, 2003). The stimulus for its introduction in higher education came from the Dearing Report (1997), which proposed that PDP, along with transcript recording of student achievement, should be implemented by all higher education institutions (HEIs) as the means by which personal development could be monitored and reflected upon by students.

The main purpose of PDP is for students to:

1 Understand their learning by, for example, being able to identify their type of learning preference(s) through engaging with learning style audits, effective note-taking, etc..

2 Be able to reflect on their performance, through acting on feedback

and advice from lecturers and supervising mentors (this would include written assignments and practical teaching and performance elements, engaging in self and peer review).

3 Plan for their future development in terms of key and professional skills and career opportunities by setting themselves targets based on personal reflection; also, engaging in research aligned to the requirements for obtaining qualified teacher status (QTS), newly qualified teacher (NQT) status, reflective practice, performance management and continuing professional development.

Through engagement in this process, students are enabled to:

- Become more effective, independent and confident self-directed learners.
- Understand how they are learning and relate their learning to a wider context.
- Improve their general skills for study and career management.
- Articulate personal goals and evaluate progress towards their achievement.
- Develop a positive attitude to learning throughout life.

(HLST, 2005, p. 3)

It is vital for students in higher education to realise the importance of PDP within a long-term plan for developing skills that will be utilised in addressing the standards for QTS and towards the production of their Career Entry and Development Profile prior to their first teaching appointment. PDP should also impact on an NQT year and on continuing professional development.

See also: *Continuing Professional Development (CPD), Reflective Practice*

FURTHER READING
Skills4Study (PDP) at www.palgrave.com/skills4study/pdp

PERIODISATION
If training is to be effective then there has to be a methodical and systematic approach to the design of training programmes to ensure that the athlete

131

reaches optimum levels of performance (peaks) at the required point of the competitive season. In order to achieve this, the athlete's training year or 'macrocycle' is divided up into a series of sub-components or 'mesocyles' (which may in turn be further split into microcycles). Each of these meso-cycles has specific training objectives appropriate to the phase of training and the particular requirements of the athlete's development at that point. This sub-dividing of the training year or 'periodisation' also means that the progress of the athlete can be monitored effectively and over-training can be avoided through the careful regulation of the volume, frequency, intensity and recovery of training.

There are different methods of periodisation, the most commonly used being the single periodised year and the double periodised year. Athletes who have indoor and outdoor seasons each competitive year (as in athletics, for example) may be required to peak several times a year, in which case a double periodised year is beneficial. The advantage of a single periodised year is the long preparation phase or 'training to train' phase providing a sound fitness base (Jones, 1990).

Wilmore and Costill (2004) suggest that in a five-phase single period-ised year, the first phase has many repetitions and sets (high volume) and low intensity. The following three phases see a decrease in volume and an increase in intensity. The final recovery phase is characterised by light resistance work or unrelated activity to promote recovery and rest prior to the start of a new cycle of training.

Table P.1: Simplified Single and Double Periodised Year for Athletics

Single

Month	Nov	Dec	Jan	Feb	Mar	April	May	Jun	Jul	Aug	Sept	Oct
Period	Preparation						Competition					Transition

Double

Month	Nov	Dec	Jan	Feb	Mar	April	May	Jun	Jul	Aug	Sept	Oct
Period	Preparation 1			Competition 1			Preparation 2			Competition 2		Transition

FURTHER READING

Wilmore, J.H. & Costill, D.L., *Physiology of Sport and Exercise* (Human Kinetics, 2004)

PHYSICAL EDUCATION AND SCHOOL SPORT CLUB LINKS (PESSCL)

see Physical Education and Sport Strategy for Young People (PESSYP)

PHYSICAL EDUCATION AND SPORT STRATEGY FOR YOUNG PEOPLE (PESSYP)

Physical Education and School Sport Club Links (PESSCL) refers to a National School Sport Strategy launched by Prime Minister Blair in October 2002. At the same time, the Department for Education and Skills (DfES) in conjunction with the Department for Culture, Media and Sport (DCMS) devised 'Learning through PE and Sport' (2003), which provided an awareness of how PESSCL aims were to be achieved. Further to this the DfES and DCMS (2004) published 'High Quality PE and Sport for Young People' (*see High Quality Physical Education*), which was a guide on how to achieve desired outcomes. Another supportive document, 'Do you have High Quality PE and School Sport in your School? (DfES, 2005)', allowed individuals to assess the quality of their PESS provision, encouraging self-evaluation by reflecting upon the ten high quality outcomes. The sum total of these documents represents the first real attempt by the government to reverse the decline in school sport since the 1950s (Armour & Kirk in Houlihan, ed., 2008). The motives behind this revised interest probably centre on concerns regarding children's health, obesity levels and perceived changes in exercise patterns. In terms of policy, however, the use of such terms as 'sport' and 'club links' represents a government desire to achieve a coordinated approach towards youth sport.

The DfES at the time worked in conjunction with the DCMS, both of whom were jointly responsible for the implementation of the PESSCL strategy, striving to meet the desired, yet ambitious, Public Service Agreement (PSA) (*see Public Service Agreement*). The primary focus of the PESSCL initiative aimed to enhance the take-up of sporting opportunities by 5–16-year-olds. The stated objective was to increase the percentage of

P

133

school children in England who spend a minimum of two hours each week on high quality PE and school sport within and beyond the curriculum to 75 per cent by 2006. PESSCL was delivered through eight strands (see Figure P.1) using the existing infrastructure of SSPs.

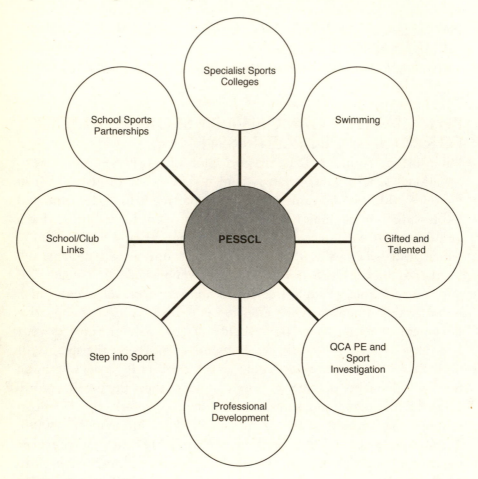

Figure P.1:

Ofsted (2009) reported on the impact of PESSCL by suggesting that this was one of the reasons for increased participation in after school activities. Due to the initial success of PESSCL the PSA target rose from 75 per cent in 2006 to an expected 85 per cent by 2008, with the government implementing further investment into the initiative, aiming to provide children with four hours of 'High Quality PE and School Sport' by the end of the decade (DfES/DCMS, 2005). Despite this apparent success within school age groups, concerns have been raised regarding the amount of sustainable provision and sporting opportunities offered for young people to engage in after secondary education has finished (Green, 2008). This has resulted in Ofsted (2009) making a recommendation to the Department for Culture, Schools and Families (DCSF) outlining a further need for provision in this age group.

Following PESSCL, the government introduced the Physical Education and Sport Strategy for Young People (PESSYP) in 2008. PESSYP built upon principles established by PESSCL and extended provision to include further education students. Further education sports coordinators (FESCOs) (*see separate entry*) have been implemented in further education colleges to provide extra opportunities for young people aged

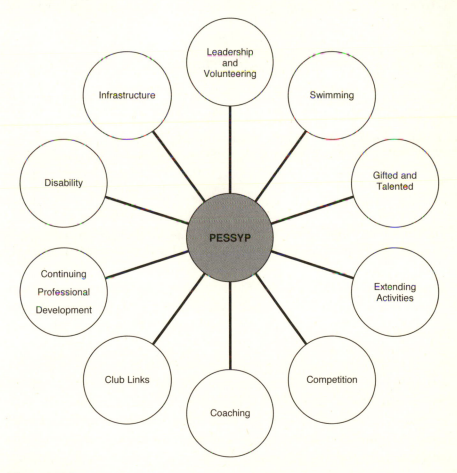

Figure P.2:

16–19 to engage in physical activity and sport. The overriding objective behind PESSYP is to implement and deliver the 'five-hour offer'. This aims to offer all children and young people five hours of high quality physical activity per week. Two hours of PE should be provided within NCPE and a further three hours may be offered beyond the curriculum by schools, community and club providers, supported by the YST and Sport England. Within further education colleges there is no statutory curriculum time dedicated to PE, therefore the target is for a three-hour offer. Again, similar to PESSCL, PESSYP is a product of joint government department collaboration, this time between the DCMS and DCSF (replacing the DfES) through ten working strands (see Figure P.2).

The YST and Sport England publish updates via a bulletin on the YST website, providing current information on the strands within the PESSYP initiative.

See also: *Government, High Quality Physical Education, Public Service Agreement (PSA)*

FURTHER READING

Armour, K. & Kirk, D., 'Physical Education and School Sport' in Houlihan, B., ed., *Sport and Society: A Student Introduction* (2nd edn, Sage, 2008), pp. 255–283

Department for Education and Skills (DfES)/Department for Culture, Media and Sport (DCMS), *Learning Through PE and Sport: A Guide to the Physical Education, School Sport and Club Links Strategy* (DfES, 2003)

Department for Education and Skills (DfES)/Department for Culture, Media and Sport (DCMS), *High Quality PE and Sport for Young People: A Guide to Recognising and Achieving High Quality PE and Sport in Schools and Clubs* (DfES, 2004)

PHILOSOPHY OF TEACHING

A philosophy of teaching statement is a narrative that includes a conception of teaching and learning, a description of how to teach, and a rationale for teaching in that particular way (Chism, 1998). This allows for teachers to evaluate their performance and justify to themselves (and their students) why they use various styles and strategies to facilitate pupil learning. It also serves as a useful aid in developing thinking about the subject in question, and teaching and learning in general. Green (2008) outlines that a philosophy broadly centres around principles underlying a knowledge base, saying that when teachers talk about 'how things should be', then they are not making use of the term philosophy in an academic sense, but more what is considered to be the essential characteristics concerning the nature of the subject and what might be termed as their world views.

Teaching is embedded in beliefs about the best ways in which the pupils should learn, and that these are part of broader beliefs about how learning takes place (Tsangaridou in Kirk et al., eds., 2006). These tend to fall somewhere on a continuum of behaviourist transmission-type learning through to constructivist theories where pupils construct understanding for themselves. The epistemological standpoint that teachers may (unconsciously) hold will be linked to how they aspire to teach (Rink, 2001).

The beliefs that teachers of physical education hold tend to be based upon what their conception of PE is, and Green (2008) links this to three areas. First, *acculturation* – childhood experiences of movement, activities, sports and physical education in school which may have an impact on beliefs, and shape attitudes for life. Studying PE at degree level may allow for, second, *professional socialisation* and this can create conflict between previously held beliefs, or cause them to be questioned. However, probably the biggest influence on how the physical educator feels about their subject will come from colleagues when they start work in schools. Here, the teacher's beliefs may be adjusted by the ethos of the school and the department. Indeed, being a part of this context may lead to reinforcement of their beliefs, or changes in their views and in their practice. This is known as the third area of belief: *occupational socialisation.*

Some of the key areas that have been identified as central to a PE teacher's beliefs and philosophies have been identified (Green in Bailey & Kirk, eds., 2009; Tsangaridou in Kirk et al., eds., 2006) as:

- **Sport:** with a focus upon competition and excellence in performance.
- **Health:** where the lifestyles of pupils beyond school are taken into account in the teaching.
- **Sport for all:** where the emphasis is on including everyone to be able to participate at their own level and taking into account inclusion.

P

- **Education for leisure:** where pupils can see the links between what they are doing and lifelong participation.
- **Enjoyment:** which has also been identified as a philosophy. While this is commendable, a rationale solely based on this would appear to undermine physical education as an academic subject, although some physical educators do not see a problem with this.

Chism (1998) highlighted essential areas that need to be taken into account when constructing a teaching philosophy. By conceptualising teaching and learning, the teacher is identifying how learning takes place and forming an understanding of the teaching styles and strategies that will allow the pupils to learn in identified ways. This links to the teacher's epistemological standpoint, and it should allow the teacher to see whether alignment between how they feel about learning and how they actually teach is taking place.

Teachers need to set goals for their students, and a teaching philosophy statement will identify what it is exactly that the teacher wants from their pupils in terms of learning outcomes. To allow for these outcomes to take place, a philosophy statement will aid the teacher in constructing problems for their pupils to solve along with clear strategies so that the pupils are aware of how it will be achieved. Finally, a growth plan needs to be included at the end, as it allows for the teachers to be able to evaluate where they have reached, and what they must do to continually progress.

See also: *Behaviourism, Constructivism, Pedagogy, Teaching Strategy*

FURTHER READING

Chism, N., *Guidance on Writing a Philosophy of Teaching Statement* (2008), available online at: www.ftad.osu.edu/portfolio/philosophy/Phil_guidance.html (accessed October 2009)

Green, K., *Physical Education Teachers on Physical Education: A Sociological Study of Philosophies and Ideologies* (Chester Academic Press, 2003)

Green, K., 'Exploring the Everyday "Philosophies" of Physical Education Teachers from a Sociological Perspective' in Bailey, R. & Kirk, D., eds., *The Routledge Physical Education Reader* (Routledge, 2009), pp. 183–205

PHYSICAL ACTIVITY

This is bodily movement resulting in energy expenditure produced by skeletal muscles. The term has mechanical, physiological and behavioural aspects. Furthermore, physical activity consists of components that are not mutually exclusive and are termed correlates: personal and demographic, psychological, social and environmental (Biddle & Mutrie, 2008). There are three approaches to the study of physical activity. The first looks at comparisons between active and inactive populations, while the second is experimental, using intervention strategies often involving a treatment group and a control group. Third, a correlational approach can be taken whereby a relationship is sought between physical activity and an indicator of growth, maturity and performance, for example fat measurements.

Patterns of physical activity participation differ between young children and adolescents. In the three to ten year age group it is often spontaneous, intermittent and non-organised. For adolescents, physical activity tends to be more organised and longer in duration (Malina et al., 2004). The levels of engagement tend to decline with age and some researchers suggest that this could begin as early as six years old (Saris et al. in Malina et al., 2004). Similarly, attendance and participation in PE lessons also declines with age (Centers for Disease Control and Prevention in Malina et al., 2004). Evidence for correlates between physical activity levels at adolescence and the middle-aged adult years is mixed (Malina et al., 2004), although there is some support for the idea that engaging in physical activity in childhood could carry over into adulthood (Biddle & Mutrie, 2008). These are important considerations given that many PE programmes desire to produce lifelong participation. Generally, however, due to difficulties in finding appropriate methods and indicators, tracking physical activity throughout different age groups remains somewhat problematic (Malina et al., 2004).

Factors that influence physical activity levels in children and adolescents include aspects of the social environment such as peer group and family influences. Research on family influences such as parental and sibling attitude towards physical activity is mixed at present as is the role of adults generally, including that of teachers. Less well documented is the role of growth and maturation although there are suggestions that some developing teenagers construct a body image which can result in less participation (Boreham & Riddoch, 2001).

P

The positive effects of activity include changes in body weight, specifically a reduction in fat levels, and improvements in skeletal development leading to improved bone density. Coakley & White (in Biddle & Mutrie, 2008) suggest that one of the barriers to the 13–23-year-old age group taking part in physical activity included a memory of negative experiences in school PE lessons. Specific instances included feelings of boredom, incompetence, lack of personal choice and criticism from peer groups. This is once again a salutary reminder to everyone in the PE profession of the responsibilities faced by all those who have an input to school-based programmes.

See also: *Growth*

Table P.2: Physical Activity Guidelines for Young People

Source	Age group	Guidelines
Sallis & Patrick, 1994	Adolescents	All adolescents should be physically active daily, or nearly every day, as part of play, games, sports, work, transportation, recreation, physical education, or planned exercise, in the context of family, school and community activities. Adolescents should engage in three or more sessions per week of activities that last 20 minutes or more at a time and that require moderate-to-vigorous levels of exertion.
Biddle et al.	5–18-year-olds	*Primary recommendation* All young people should participate in physical activity of at least moderate intensity for one hour per day. Young people who currently do little activity should participate in physical activity of at least half an hour per day. *Secondary recommendation* At least twice per week, some of these activities should help to enhance and maintain muscular strength and flexibility, and bone health.

Source: taken from Biddle & Mutrie (2008)

FURTHER READING

Biddle, S. & Mutrie, N., *Psychology of Physical Activity* (2nd edn, Routledge, 2008)

Malina, R., Bouchard, C. & Bar-Or, O., *Growth, Maturation and Physical Activity* (2nd edn, Human Kinetics, 2004)

PHYSICAL EDUCATION

This school curriculum subject has been the cause of considerable contestation and discourse (*see Discourse*) over many years. PE has become socially constructed whereby different pedagogies, forms of knowledge and assessment strategies are selected to fit the needs of various interest groups, whether they be from sport, education or health. Historically, however, the popular viewpoint has been to promote an inclusive ideology underpinning PE in schools with a desire to protect it from becoming engulfed by sport (Kay, 2003). Furthermore, the instrumental values behind PE include the inculcation of physical skills sometimes within a health-based setting. Preparation for leisure is considered vital alongside the acquisition of humanistic values such as morality, leadership and codes of behaviour. PE should be delivered by trained teachers based on a curriculum that has breadth and depth. Activities should be fun, enjoyable and offered within a safe and supportive environment. The aim then is to improve the quality of life based on aesthetic appreciation leading to creative performance.

This can contrast strongly with *sport* which is a more formalised pattern of behaviours involving serious play in an institutionalised setting. Sport is also concerned with performance; it is the test of a person's natural abilities and the limitations that can come with that. Success can lead to improved self-worth, while failure can lead to feelings of rejection, exclusion and ultimately elimination. Active participation in PE, though, should take account of an individual's social and emotional well-being. It should promote feelings of security and success leading to greater self-esteem, in order to improve the quality of learning. To achieve this PE lessons should celebrate improvement to a greater extent than performance. A good example of this can be found in timed activities such as cross-country running, where improvements based on previous scores can be noted rather than ranked positions in a race.

p

The concepts behind sport will be found within many PE curriculums but need to be kept in moderation; 'Sport . . . is a component of physical education not vice-versa' (Kay, 2006, p. 27).

As the term *school sport* has become increasingly prevalent within government initiatives in recent years, so the debate between sport and PE has intensified. Kay (2003) believes that the PE profession should be wary of the language and discourse used within terms such as sports colleges and school sport coordinators. There is a fear here that teaching may become replaced by coaching and that school PE lessons may be serviced by a government desire to discover talent. Bailey (2005) suggests that sport itself is a term that can be accepted more readily by the PE profession if it can lead to greater public understanding and perhaps even, ultimately, a stronger political position. Armour & Kirk (in Houlihan, ed., 2008) even suggest that by adopting the term physical education and school sport (PESS) a clear message was being sent out to politicians that the 'war' between the two terms was over. Generally, there is an acceptance now that it is PE that takes place within curriculum time while school sport refers to those physical activities that take place outside of the normal school day (Ofsted, 2004).

FURTHER READING

Bailey, R., 'Words and Things: A Response to Will Kay', *Bulletin of Physical Education,* 41 (2) (2005), pp. 163–166

Kay, W., 'Physical Education, R.I.P.?', *British Journal Of Teaching Physical Education,* Winter (2003), pp. 6–10

PHYSICAL LITERACY

This is a concept developed as a 'statement of intent' for lifelong physical achievement and competency. Proposed by a PE lecturer named Margaret Whitehead in 2001, it utilised previous ideas concerning child development (Maude, 2001) and formulated a process for PE teachers to work towards in the quest for the holistic physical development of an individual. Thus, physically literate individuals are those whose movement is characterised by poise, economy and confidence. They can respond to a variety of physically challenging situations and are perceptive in interpreting the environment. Underpinning the whole process is a strong personal motivation – almost a drive to succeed.

Whitehead (2001) expresses concern as to whether physical literacy can be culturally confined, limited to specific musculature and perhaps lack adaptations for the physically challenged. Nevertheless, she has identified four key areas within the concept: first, reference is made to embodied capacities, which are essentially the basic components of health- and skill-related fitness necessary to carry out a wide range of movement skills; second, a physically literate individual needs to respond towards a range of environmental situations; third, creative skills need to be developed in settings where self-presentation and non-verbal communication are important; and fourth, there is a need to display the perception necessary to interpret different situations using in particular previous experience and knowledge. Generally, physical literacy promotes the idea that each person has their own physical potential and that a PE programme should then reflect this in its range and content of activities. To acquire it a child needs to be able to perform basic movement competencies, which need to be applied in a number of settings. Self-evaluation is important in order to progress, along with developing an independence and displaying strong internal motivation.

Haydn-Davies (2005) promotes physical literacy as part of the need for lifelong physical activity. Similarly, Whitehead & Murdoch (2006) suggest that there are six stages involved, which start at birth and progress until old age. Haydn-Davies (2005) has also noted how the concept matches in part the DfES/DCMS statement of high quality outcomes in PE (2003). Furthermore, the need for a diverse range of activities in the PE curriculum along with the pursuit of knowledge, skills and understanding within a supportive pedagogical framework perhaps contrasts the outcomes of sport. This lends credence to the concern that the principles behind physical literacy clash with government ideology used within the current elevation of PESS. Consequently, the debate surrounding physical literacy may well have been relegated by competing agendas. However, the drive towards improving the nation's health may well necessitate a re-examination of curriculum content if children are to be attracted towards physical activity as a lifelong process.

Despite their initial enthusiasm, proponents of physical literacy do have concerns with regard to its universal acceptance by the PE profession as an appropriate concept. Whitehead (www.physical-literacy.org.uk) refers to how cultural factors interfere particularly with regard to a male hegemony *(see Hegemony)* which emphasises the physical performance side of PE rather than the non-physical, such as creative, social, cognitive and personal aspects. However, physical literacy is there as a concept for PE teachers to know what they are aiming for both in terms of process and outcome. It should be viewed as part of the lifelong holistic development of the individual with PE making a vital contribution along the way.

See also: *Fundamental Movement Skills, Gifted and Talented*

FURTHER READING
www.physical-literacy.org.uk

PHYSIOLOGY (EXERCISE AND SPORT)

Exercise and sport physiology developed from the origins of anatomy and physiology, which in turn can be traced back to the ancient world and the work of physicians such as Herophilus (335–280 BC), Herodicus (484 BC) and Hippocrates (460–377 BC) in ancient Greece (*see Ancient Greeks*), and Galen (AD 131–201) in ancient Rome. Anatomy is the study of the structure of the body, whereas physiology is concerned with the functioning of the body systems from system level (a collection of organs that work together to achieve a common outcome, e.g. digestive system) down to the sub-cellular chemical reactions that take place in biochemistry (the study of the chemical reactions in living things, e.g. cellular respiration).

Exercise and sport physiologists, as with sports psychologists and biomechanists, endeavour to use scientific knowledge and techniques to enhance performance in sport and physical activity. Many of the top athletes in the world, for example, will have access to exercise and sport physiology support. Exercise and sport physiologists 'study how the body's structure and function are altered when we are exposed to acute and chronic bouts of exercise' (Wilmore & Costill, 2004, p. 3). An important role of the physiologist is to look at scientific methods of maximising performance potential through training. This might include looking at training regimes, preparation for performance in varying climatic conditions such as altitude and humidity, and observing physiological responses to training programmes, e.g. anaerobic threshold and lactate accumulation.

In terms of teaching PE, an underpinning understanding of basic physiological processes is important. Knowledge of the physical development of children, for example, will inform an awareness of appropriate levels of physical activity at different stages of pupil development. As a teacher of PE, you will be required to understand how the body functions, responds and adapts to exercise and be able to develop this understanding in your students. This is particularly the case when delivering theoretical components of recognised award-bearing courses such as GCSE and A Level physical education, where anatomy and physiology are key components in many cases.

FURTHER READING

Kirk, D., Cooke, C., Flintoff, A. & McKenna, J., *Key Concepts in Sport and Exercise Sciences* (Sage, 2008)

Wilmore, J.H. & Costill, D.L., *Physiology of Sport and Exercise* (Human Kinetics, 2004)

PLANNING

This is a vital skill for teachers to acquire: a cognitive process that looks at objectives, content, assessment, teaching strategies and differentiation. Planning by the teacher in itself won't guarantee pupil learning but will make it more likely. Those teachers who are skilful planners are usually more effective in influencing factors involving equipment, feedback, progression and the pace of PE lessons. Planning can take place at different times for teachers. Before a lesson takes place there is a need to visualise and to think ahead; even while delivering teachers need to plan and adapt, especially for the unexpected. Afterwards, self-evaluation is important to inform future planning.

There are different levels of planning, which are usually based on the timescales under review. So, short-term considerations involve looking at a lesson plan, medium term can refer to a unit frame, while long-term planning concentrates on a scheme of work. Clark & Yinger (in Macfadyen & Bailey, 2002, p. 87) call this a 'nested process' (see Figure P.3). Here, they suggest that specific tasks are embedded at all levels of planning and teachers need to understand how each layer will relate to the others. The factors to consider are numerous and can perhaps be summarised under concerns involving resources and pedagogical considerations. Some less obvious issues include planning for learning across the curriculum involving social, moral, spiritual and cultural aspects. Other factors some-times neglected include planning for transitions within lessons and making available tasks for non-participants in PE.

Planning for progression in PE has been highlighted as a cause for concern (QCA, 2005). Failure to provide content that builds upon and links with that which has preceded it and a failure to increase the level

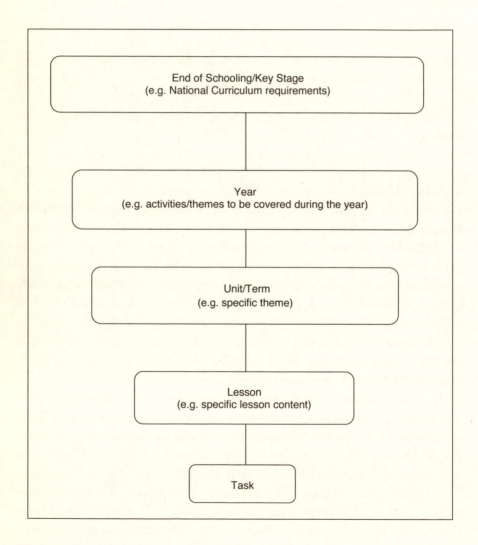

Figure P.3: Planning As a Nested Process (from Macfadyen & Bailey, 2002)

of difficulty and challenge appropriate for specific abilities can lead to pupil boredom and ultimately disaffection. To alleviate these problems, Siedentop (1991) suggests that teachers can improve progression by looking at the final desired outcome from a unit of work and then move in reverse to the very first lesson. Furthermore, SCCA (1995) recommend reinforcing and consolidating themes as a form of curriculum coherence by looking at how different activities can relate to each other. Finally, Williams (1996) highlights the qualities that are required for effective progression by looking at the levels of difficulty, responses and contexts involved when tasks are set in PE.

Effective planning in PE teachers can be a reflection of age and experience. Here, there is a suggestion that younger teachers plan for activity based on a linear approach, while experienced teachers consider the needs of their pupils. The ability to adapt is crucial. Experienced teachers are particularly adept at continually assessing situations and having a number of contingency plans available for scenarios involving resources, pupil cognition and pupil discipline. Experienced teachers are also particularly insistent on obtaining information regarding resources and pupils' needs before planning takes place. Griffey & Housner (in Hardy & Mawer, eds., 1999) are sympathetic towards what they refer to as the dilemma facing beginner teachers – how can they plan for situations that they are not familiar with? There is a recognition that planning can then become superficial, based on a need for pupil compliance and conformity and ultimately leading to a form of didactic teaching. Similarly, Macfadyen & Bailey (2002) have noticed how beginner teachers often begrudge having to write out detailed lesson plans while more mature colleagues seem to rely on less prescriptive methods. However, such an observation perhaps belies the fact that with more experienced teachers effective planning is still taking place. While younger teachers may find short-term planning in the written form something of a chore they should be mindful of the fact that they are continually reinforcing concepts and procedures which will stand them in good stead throughout their careers. Planning is a skill that will require a lot of hard work at first but will reap rich dividends later on. A good example for beginner PE teachers is to make an inventory concerning the amount of sports equipment that is available to them along with a drawn plan of the school gym/sports hall showing all marked lines and spaces. Such information will help in the construction of lesson plans.

P

An up-to-date personal diary is also essential to record forthcoming meetings and inter-school fixtures.

FURTHER READING

Hardy, C.A. & Mawer, M., eds., *Learning and Teaching in Physical Education* (RoutledgeFalmer, 1999)

Macfadyen, T. & Bailey, R., *Teaching Physical Education 11–18* (Continuum, 2002)

PLAY

The concept of 'play' is found in activities that are characterised by time, space, fun, spontaneity and, most importantly, intrinsic values. It is a worthwhile pastime in itself and is not enacted for any external reward; it is there for pure pleasure. Play is an important constituent in sport and should be part of a good PE lesson.

A philosopher named Huizinga (1949) stressed the importance of play, stating that its relevance is on a par with nutrition, reproduction and self-preservation. Huizinga (ibid.) also placed great emphasis on the fun aspect of play, something which many PE teachers have traditionally also seen as an important factor in their lessons (Green, 2003). While this may suggest a conflict with the more serious educative objectives, a balance between the two is surely justified. PE is in a unique position to do this given the variety of settings chosen for the subject, the variety of activities available and the potential sheer joy of partaking in exercise.

Although Huizinga (1949) saw play as non-serious, it can be significant for different age groups. Adults, then, use play to escape from their everyday lives by engaging in activities that will provide relief from the stresses and strains of work and family life. For children play can at times reinforce reality. So, although play should be an immediate source of enjoyment, this can be tempered by a realisation that through such activities a child can learn about their own physical capabilities and subsequently what their friends really think about them. Such activities as 'picking teams' before a play activity can make children feel worthless if left until last by their peers. Needless to say that a PE teacher should never allow this to happen in a school lesson.

If play involves minimal adult interference then a good PE teacher will have to think carefully on how to incorporate such activities in a lesson. A good opportunity will be at the start where simple games of 'tig' and 'tag' can be used as warm-ups. For a more cognitive task a simple game of 'dodge ball' can be used to introduce the sport of basketball. Although interference from the teacher should be kept to a minimum, the teacher can stop the activity at various points and explain the rules of travelling and double dribble. There will also be opportunities to emphasise the value of game concepts such as passing and support.

FURTHER READING
Huizinga, J., *Homo Ludens* (Routledge, 1949)

POLICY
A subject of concern for some physical educationists who see the plethora of government initiatives as leading to a 'crowded arena' (Houlihan, 2000) involving too many external agencies (Green, 2008). Others warn of competing sectors, with education, sport and health all striving to find a voice through PE (Talbot, 2008). In fact, it is possible to suggest that separate policies for PE and school sport are now intertwined and that any conflict between the two is being won by the latter (King, 2009).

Policy is perhaps best viewed as a 'statement of intent regarding maintaining, modifying or achieving something' (Green, 2008, p. 23). It can begin as an issue and lead to an authority statement on how things should be. Policy can be a process of reification, created by some people and implemented by others. *Agency* and *structure* can be involved when addressing issues of power such as in the school target-setting process for students' grades, where interference can be found at a number of levels. Here, a teacher's autonomy in this process can be undermined by influence from a school's senior management team, who in turn can feel under pressure from the local authority to amend targets. Penny & Evans (in Green & Hardman, eds., 2005) contend that policy can sometimes be initiated just for the sake of it: 'policy is continually made and remade' (p. 24). The suggestion, then, is that successive pedagogical documents have led to a curriculum that hasn't really changed that much over the years. Furthermore, the implementation gap between theory and practice has led

P

to 'slippage' (Penny & Evans in Green & Hardman, eds., 2005) whereby official texts are read and then activated in a different manner from that which was originally intended.

Recent policies have made extravagant claims concerning the ability of PE to improve people's health and well-being (PESSCL, 2003). There is also the suggestion that the latter initiative has too many aims, some of which are incompatible, and that the involvement of too many external agencies such as NGBs could lead to a situation where PE teachers feel threatened and even undermined. Future concerns for PE policy also highlight the consultation process. Are teachers views really considered within a subject that has undoubtedly been the focus of much attention and finance in recent years?

With regard to school sport policy, Houlihan (in King, 2009) states that there are three 'clusters' of interests that survive to this day. These are core beliefs held by policy actors, which include: first, those concerned with pedagogical interests and who represent the education community; second, there are those who represent the organisation and administration of sport, especially at elite level; and third, the interests of youth work and play are held by those who are only indirectly concerned with school sport. All three are potential stakeholders constrained by competing objectives that shape school sport policy. The first of these concerns the politics of education and centres on teacher status, which is closely linked to the continuing discourse over the place of sport and PE within the school curriculum. The final competing objective relates to the administration of school sport where several government departments have varying levels of responsibility and impact (*see Government*). King (2009) suggests that all interests within this sphere are governed by issues concerning acquisition and competition for resources and organisational survival.

FURTHER READING

Green, K., *Understanding Physical Education* (Sage, 2008)

Green, K. & Hardman, K., eds., *Physical Education: Essential Issues* (Sage, 2005)

Houlihan, B., 'Sporting Excellence, Schools and Sports Development: The Politics of Crowded Policy Spaces', *European Physical Education Review*, 6 (2) (2000), pp. 171–193

King, N., *Sport Policy and Governance: Local Perspectives* (Elsevier, 2009)

Talbot, M., 'Valuing Physical Education: Package or Pedagogy?', *Physical Education Matters,* 3 (3) (2008), pp. 6–8

PRIMARY LINK TEACHERS (PLTS)

These are existing primary school teachers given the responsibility of improving PESS within their own particular institution. Created as part of the PESSCL strategy, PLTs liaise with SSCOs and the SSP to help drive through both local and national initiatives. They are part of the government's response to the widely held view that PE in primary schools has traditionally failed to provide high quality teaching due to a lack of knowledge among teachers and a lack of resources (Green, 2008).

In fact, Ofsted (2009) has suggested that there has been a recent marked improvement within PE in primary schools. The PESSCL initiative in particular has perhaps benefited the latter more than secondary schools in terms of both increased participation and resources. Thus, Small & Nash (in Green, 2008) report on how the TOPS programme (YST-funded free equipment and continuing professional development for teachers) within their locality has led to improved resources for primary schools. However, Green (2008) believes that externally provided resources such as this can create new PE programmes within themselves and so provide an example of unwarranted outside interference. Ofsted (2009) also reported on the perceived benefits of continuing CPD for PLTs. The 12 days a year training allowance had enabled an awareness of roles and responsibilities leading to improved management skills and increased subject knowledge. Generally, it was felt that CPD within PE for primary teachers had led to improvements in teaching and subsequently pupil attainment.

Despite the impact of PESSCL, Ofsted (2009) found that the standard of PE teaching within primary schools was variable when compared to secondary schools; this was often ascribed to a lack of subject knowledge, attributed in turn to a lack of professional development at ITE level. The quality of facilities and resources at primary school level was also found to be variable, although leadership (*see separate entry*) opportunities, such as through the Sport Education programme, within PE for pupils in years 5 and 6 had increased.

P

151

Green (2008) suggests that PE is still marginalised in primary schools. He maintains that despite recent initiatives, or even possibly because of them, teachers are still confused as to who has responsibility for the subject. Is it the primary-based PLT or the sports-college-based SSCO? Furthermore, a research group termed the Loughborough Partnership (2009) revealed that the appointment and turnover among PLTs is a concern for most SSPs. The same source also reports problems with communication within this structure, citing the fact that 33 per cent of PLTs researched did not know if they had a competition manager or not. The continued lack of specialist teachers in primary schools and the reliance on coaches to assist the PE programme is also put forward to supplement this concern. Green (2008) even goes as far as to say that 'PE is treated more like "play" than an introduction to particular sporting activities' (p. 56).

Nevertheless, a considered view based on the latest evidence put forward by Ofsted (2009) would suggest that recent improvements within PE in primary schools have taken place. To make comparisons with the situation in secondary schools is unfair given the vast differences in resources available for the subject between the two. Primary schools are important for introducing the principles and values of PE and it is hoped that with the assistance of recent government initiatives the subject will continue to progress within this setting.

See also: *Partnership Development Manager (PDM)*, *Physical Education and Sport Strategy for Young People (PESSYP)*, *School Sports Colleges (SSCS)*, *School Sports Coordinator (SSCO)*

FURTHER READING

Green, K., *Understanding Physical Education* (Sage, 2008)

Office for Standards in Education (Ofsted), *Physical Education in Schools 2005/08* (Ofsted, 2009)

PROFESSIONAL STANDARDS FOR TEACHERS

This is a set of standards which contain statements of teachers' professional attributes, knowledge, understanding and skills. The standards are underpinned by the five 'Every Child Matters' key outcomes. The framework consists of standards covering the various stages of a teacher's career development, clearly outlining the expectations at each career stage:

- The award of qualified teacher status (QTS)   Q
- Teachers on the main scale (core)   C
- Teachers on the upper pay scale (post-threshold teachers) P
- Excellent teachers   E
- Advanced skills teachers (ASTs)   A

Each set of standards within the framework are arranged into three areas: professional attributes, professional knowledge and understanding, and professional skills. In order to access the various stages, teachers need to demonstrate that they have met the relevant standards. They are also beneficial in assisting teachers with their CPD requirements in being able to ensure teachers can clearly identify the requirements for progression. This can be aligned with the performance management process where teachers can review their performance and set targets for future development.

To be recommended for qualified teacher status (QTS), individuals must have undertaken a course (such as a PGCE or degree with QTS) with an accredited Initial Teacher Training (ITT) provider and have been successfully assessed against all of the standards for QTS. The 'professional attributes' section of the QTS standards emphasises to undergraduate physical education students the benefits of early engagement with the PDP process (*see Personal Development Planning*) and how it helps to develop required skills and prepare for subsequent personal professional reflection and development. For example, they are expected to be able to 'communicate effectively . . . ' (Q4), commit to 'collaboration and cooperative working' (Q6), 'reflect on and improve their practice, and take responsibility for identifying and meeting their developing professional needs' (Q7a) and 'act upon advice and feedback . . . ' (TDA, 2007, pp. 7–8). In order to achieve QTS, standard Q16 also identifies that the trainee must have successfully 'passed the professional skills tests in numeracy, literacy and ICT' (TDA, 2007, p. 9), again reinforcing the importance of key skills development through their undergraduate course and the professional expectations and requirements for these skills subsequently in their career.

P

FURTHER READING

The Training and Development Agency for Schools (TDA) at www.tda. gov.uk/standards

PUBLIC SERVICE AGREEMENT (PSA)

Public Service Agreements (PSAs) highlight government priority outcomes and are imperative in enhancing their delivery to the general public in order to maximise opportunities for participation. There are 30 PSAs in total and the PSA concerned with PESSYP is PSA 22. This is lead by the DCMS and is entwined with aims and objectives for delivering a successful Olympics and Paralympics in 2012. Each PSA has supporting 'indicators' that act as criteria for success in order to achieve the desired outcome. PSA 22 contributes towards the government's vision of promoting physical activity as a lifelong process. In adherence to PESSYP specific reference can be drawn upon Indicator Five as this focuses upon 'creation of a world class system for Physical Education and Sport'. In fact, it is this indicator that has undoubtedly underpinned the ideology surrounding PESSYP.

See also: *Physical Education and Sport Strategy for Young People (PESSYP)*

r

RATIONAL RECREATION

The term arising from a period in the late 19th and early 20th centuries when organised sport really did develop at an extraordinary rate. Games became codified, NGBs were established and the period witnessed a big growth in spectator sport.

The rapid industrialisation of Britain signified a move towards an urban society and an expansion in the transport system became useful in the development of inter-town sporting rivalry. A new middle class had emerged who were often employed as managers in many of the new factories, some of whom had attended the English public schools. It was the attempts of the bourgeoisie to introduce sport to the masses, and subsequent resistance within some sectors, which formed part of a perceived ongoing class struggle that lasted well into the 20th century (Hargreaves, 1986).

Undoubtedly, then, Rational Recreation was in part the result of the attempts made to spread public school athleticism throughout society and indeed the British Empire. The ex-public school boys graduated from the universities and transmitted their interest in games via their new posts as clerics, industrialists, school teachers and military personnel. Closely allied with the concept of Muscular Christianity as a means of combining both physical and spiritual development, the motives for doing so are a subject of debate. The more enlightened perhaps did so for philanthropic reasons as shown by the opening of 'settlements' in major industrial cities. Some historians suggest that sport was encouraged by factory owners as a means of social control and that this notion links in well with Gramsci's theory of hegemony (1971 – *see separate entry*). Indeed, many sports clubs formed during this period were merely a social extension of the workplace.

Working-class reaction towards middle-class attempts to impose structure on their leisure time depended upon locality and the sport in question. Hargreaves (1986) suggests that workers adapted and adopted in their own way. A split became apparent between skilled and unskilled, with the latter often discouraged by the former within the aim of working towards middle-class respectability. The bourgeoisie became vigilant, especially in a sport like football, which soon found a ready acceptance among the working classes. The reaction here from the latter was to influence some measure of control by using commercial influence in the form of brewery sponsorship. Generally, however, whatever the complexities of the period, what is not in doubt is that there was an unprecedented growth in the organisation and acceptance of sport across all social classes.

See also: *Athleticism*

FURTHER READING

Hargreaves, J., *Sport, Power and Culture: A Social and Historical Analysis of Popular Sports in Britain* (Polity Press, 1986)

Tranter, N., *Sport, Economy and Society in Britain 1750–1914* (Cambridge University Press, 1998)

RECREATION

Leisure activities offering time, opportunity and choice. A chance to engage in pastimes that can be both socially civilising and self-fulfilling – a response to the routine of everyday life that provides refreshment, health and enjoyment. For adults many of these activities offer opportunities to escape the drudgery of work and provide the chance to achieve and accomplish goals not offered within employment. *Physical recreation* encompasses all of these principles but also relates to physical activities involving minimal organisation often conducted in a non-competitive setting. Examples include rambling, boating and jogging, which by the very nature of the terminology selected suggest activities that are for fun, with little competition. It is a concept highly respected within some Western societies where taking part is considered as a worthy alternative to winning. Physical recreation is also valued within PESS programmes where the concepts involved can often underpin many after school activities. These are usually termed 'clubs' where pupils meet to play for fun and rarely engage in competition, as opposed to the more serious extra-curricular inter-school sport. It can also form, perhaps to a lesser extent, the basis of many intra-school competitions as well. *Outdoor recreation* builds on these definitions in the natural environment, offering personal challenge and an appreciation of the great outdoors. The more formalised, institutionalised activities in this setting such as canoeing and rock climbing are termed *outdoor pursuits.* Both of the latter two concepts have been combined in schools to create *outdoor and adventurous activities*, a term that has found favour within National Curriculum language as well.

See also: *National Curriculum*

FURTHER READING
Coakley, J., *Sport and Society: Issues and Controversies* (5th edn, Mosby, 1994)

REFLECTIVE PRACTICE

r

This involves evaluating personal teaching performance and asking questions such as 'What worked well or not so well?' and 'How could that be improved in the future?' A good teacher will undergo this process constantly in their everyday practice, considering alternative ways of doing things and generally being thoughtful about effective practice. Students are also encouraged to reflect upon an assignment and consider what has been learned from the feedback. A trainee teacher will certainly be expected to reflect upon their teaching, not merely to be able to complete the required paperwork, or to obtain marks for that process, but to genuinely develop an ability to improve practice. At this level a mentor will encourage and guide in this process to set targets in developing teaching skills and successfully addressing the 'Standards for Qualified Teacher

Status' (TDA, 2007). This ability to reflect will also be important for a 'Career Entry and Development Profile' in preparation for a first teaching appointment. However, these skills will be useful long after ITE level. Reflective practice and subsequent continuing professional development (CPD) is, as the name suggests, an ongoing process for the rest of a professional career.

A student of PE, in addition to reflecting on the development of teaching skills, should also reflect on their philosophy of the subject, developing values, beliefs and understanding (Breckon & Capel in Capel, ed., 2004). The ability to reflect on personal performance also depends on the ability to observe: to view critically the organisation of the lesson, the response and behaviour of the participants, the quality of learning taking place and whether objectives for the session were met. There is a need to 'replay' the lesson or teaching episode in the mind, noting any points of concern or 'critical incidents' and recording them, evaluating what the possible causes were and what can be done about them in future.

The process of reflection involves being able to identify an area of interest, focusing on one particular aspect of that concern and considering what can be done about it. Then there is a need to implement a strategy for improvement, evaluating evidence from it and, finally, to establish that improved professional practice has occurred (Bleach, 2001). Schon distinguished between reflection 'in' action and reflection 'on' action (Zwodiak-Myers in Capel et al., eds., 2006). Reflecting on action has formed much of what has been discussed above. Reflecting in action refers to the ability to observe the situation of the lesson, for example, as it unfolds and to judge whether objectives are being addressed or whether modifications in the teaching strategy need to be considered. An example of how successful this is can be seen from the response of the children to tasks and also through assessment methods such as pupil questioning.

FURTHER READING

Breckon, P. & Capel, S., 'Your Wider Role as a PE Teacher' in Capel, S., ed., *Learning to Teach Physical Education in the Secondary School: A Companion to School Experience* (2nd edn, RoutledgeFalmer, 2004)

Zwodiak-Myers, P., 'The Reflective Practitioner' in Capel, S., Breckon, P. & O'Neill, J., eds., *A Practical Guide to Teaching Physical Education in the Secondary School* (Routledge, 2006)

RELIABILITY/VALIDITY

Reliability in research is the quality assurance mechanism put in place by researchers in an attempt to ensure consistency within the procedures of collecting, collating and analysing data. Although Wellington (2000) maintains that this will be impossible to achieve with qualitative data because of the numerous variables involved, the researcher should still strive for reliability rather than expect to achieve it.

Working to develop the extent to which procedures produce similar results on all occasions gives the research credibility and dependability. Therefore, it is important that the methods used to collect, collate and analyse the data are gathered using conditions that are as closely matched as possible. The aim of this is to ensure that the results are consistent and repeatable across a range of settings, particularly if completed by more than one researcher. To ensure that this takes place, a test can be repeated at different times to see if the same scores are achieved, although it would be necessary to ensure that the quantity being measured wasn't changing. This may be more difficult to achieve with qualitative research. Methods such as interviewing and using questionnaires may benefit initially from using a pilot as a good mechanism in striving for reliability. This can then be evaluated to check for participant understanding, or whether the questions have lead the respondent completing the interview or questionnaire to give a particular answer.

Opie (2004) recommends looking at reliability in the use and process of gathering the data, rather than just at the data itself, as this is more likely to be consistent, and deliver what he calls 'quality research'.

There may be some concerns with regard to reliability in social research. Gratton & Jones (2005) identify three potential threats to the whole process:

1 **Subject error:** this is when the subject responds differently as a consequence of when the research is carried out. Asking a teacher about their perception of an incident directly after it has happened may provide rich data, but it may also affect what they say about it, as a later account at another time would offer completely different information. Therefore the research should be conducted at a neutral time.

2 **Researcher error:** this tends to happen when multiple researchers carry out the research and involuntarily get different responses from the subjects. An example may be that the researcher's questionnaire may not correspond to those points raised in an interview situation, and the two sets of data are not aligned with the research question.

r

159

3 **Subject bias:** this may occur when the participant gives a response that they think the researcher will want to hear. Pupils in school may offer information which they think will be the correct response if it is thought that the data will reflect personally upon them, or if the researcher is in a position of social power.

Validity is often associated with reliability, but research data can be reliable without being valid. However, if the data is unreliable, then this will affect the validity, and make the research invalid. Validity is extremely important for effective research as generally it is asking whether the research is measuring what it is supposed to measure, or to the extent that the 'truth' is actually what it is supposed to be. Indeed, Silverman (2010) suggests that validity is another word for truth. Cohen et al. (2007) also emphasise the importance of validity for effective research, but they look at it as a degree rather than as a certain state. The qualitative researcher will seek to maximise it, although the idea that there will be a certain amount of bias will be accepted. Yin (2003) highlights different types of validity that may be evident in the research process, but this is beyond the scope of undergraduate research.

Triangulation is a means of both developing validity and ensuring that the research findings are trustworthy (Thomas et al., 2005). This can take place by using different approaches to the investigation, either through collecting the data, or by looking at the situation from a variety of perspectives. These independent data sources can be used to support a conclusion. Opie (2004) also draws attention to the differences within the validity of the relationship between a claim and the results of the data-gathering processes. This would be instead of the method, test or research tool being valid on its own.

Although theories of reliability and validity need to be considered throughout all research, they tend to be of greater concern to researchers testing theories or hypotheses that are often more associated with positivism. With subjectivist-type research, ensuring the research is credible is more of a pertinent consideration.

See also: *Ethics, Informed Consent, Methodology*

FURTHER READING

Opie, C., *Doing Educational Research: A Guide to First Time Researchers* (Sage, 2004)

Wellington, J., *Educational Research: Contemporary Issues and Practical Approaches* (Continuum, 2000)

RESEARCH APPROACH

The format that research follows should be compatible with the epistemological standpoint and the methodological approach of the researcher. Very often the (epistemological) approaches taken in collecting the data are confused with the instruments (questionnaires/interviews/observations, etc.) used to gather the information (Cohen et al., 2007). It is important that the researcher is clear about what approach fits best within the research question, and also matches the context under which the investigation will be studied. To be 'fit for purpose', the research needs to be designed to enable the collection of data within the confines of both validity and reliability (Gratton & Jones, 2005).

At undergraduate level, the majority of physical education students will undertake qualitative social research through the medium of a case study. There are other research formats that could be followed such as action research, an ethnographic approach or grounded theory, but it is unlikely that undergraduate research will allow for these as there is often a limited time scale involved within the whole undergraduate research process.

A *case study* is the detailed study of a setting, an event, or a subject, and from a PE perspective this could involve a person, a group of people, a class or even a school. The object of a case study is to build up a picture of a situation and look at the factors influencing the situation to gain an understanding of it (Wellington, 2000). Opie (2004, p. 74) builds upon this by stating that '. . . the focus of a case study is on a real situation with real people in an environment often familiar to the researcher'. Different types of case study have been identified (Cohen et al., 2007), and although they adopt different procedures, the aim is to gain a holistic understanding of a set of issues and how they relate to the case(s). Examples include descriptive (as narrative accounts); interpretive (to examine assumptions); and evaluative (that explain and judge). Therefore, although it may not be easy to generalise from the findings, case studies are undertaken in order to gain a better understanding of the case, and '. . . not because the case is unique or typical, but because it is of interest in itself' (Wellington, 2000, p. 92). Some concern has been raised about a lack of rigour in case study research (Yin, 2003), particularly if large amounts of data are accrued and

161

there is little control over external factors that shape it. Bannigan (2006) points out, though, that all types of research have their strengths and weaknesses. To guard against Yin's (2003) concerns, research design, data collection techniques and approaches to the data analysis have to be thorough as he warns against both the danger of vulnerability and difficulties incurred if making wide generalisations. This is because of the problems in making generalised assumptions when so many factors can affect the data.

Action research is conducted by practitioners in order to improve or develop an aspect of their practice. For PE undergraduates, it is an opportunity to gain an understanding of something that may reflect personal involvement within a particular setting. The key aim is to bring about a change in the researcher's practice, their situation, or a system (Wellington, 2000). In small-scale research this may involve the student looking at an aspect of their teaching, evaluating it, and putting new approaches into place based upon the initial findings. The intention to change or improve is critical to action research, but for undergraduate students this is likely to be on a very small scale as there are too many limiting factors including time and the opportunity to implement the 'action'. To gain an understanding of a problem, it is important that the process starts with a period of reflection to analyse the issue. An intervention strategy is proposed and then put into place. What then has to follow is an additional period of reflection to evaluate the effectiveness of the intervention strategy. A comparison can then be drawn with the situation at the beginning of the cycle, and then, depending upon time limits, the process can begin again.

Ethnography is research that gains the perspective of a situation from the view of the people involved, rather than from the viewpoint of the researcher. The researcher needs to get an 'inside view' of natural behaviours in a natural setting (Gratton & Jones, 2005), but to be able to do this effectively, there is a need to spend extended periods of time absorbed within the group.

Grounded theory is an approach where the researcher will initially gather information, and then formulate a theory or hypothesis from the data that has been collected and collated. Subsequent research can then test the theory. The complexities of using this approach may deter undergraduate students, as data analysis can be difficult to organise due to the need for the data to be highly structured into many different codes over a period of time. As most undergraduate research is conducted in a short time span, most students would find that interpreting the codes manually would not make good use of their time, especially if they had other assessment commitments. This method often makes use of a computer programme to interpret the coding, and students would have to become familiar with the different software packages.

Finally, it should be said that researchers may use approaches within an approach, such as when an ethnographic approach could form the basis of a case study. For the majority of undergraduate students conducting research in a short space of time, a case study approach would appear to be the most sensible.

See also: *Epistemology/Ontology, Methodology, Research Methods (Data Collection)*

FURTHER READING

Cohen, L., Manion, L. & Morrison, K., *Research Methods in Education* (Routledge, 2007)

RESEARCH METHODS (DATA COLLECTION)

Undergraduate social research is usually conducted over relatively short periods of time. Research conducted by physical education students will generally be qualitative, seeking to find out opinions and perceptions of those involved in their interest area, and gathering them as either the spoken or written word (Curtner-Smith in Laker, ed., 2002). As the process is personal and interactive, the data will rely heavily on the social skills and interactive capacities of the researcher (Sparkes, 1992). Three of the most common methods of collecting data in social research are the questionnaire, the interview, and through researcher observations.

Questionnaires are effective as they can gather a great deal of data in a short space of time, and they can be structured to make the data easy to analyse and interpret. The questions can be tailored to meet the demands of the research question, and it is acceptable to keep the responses anonymous. Questionnaires tend to provide data that is factual, and according to Bell (2005) they can effectively answer questions of what, where, when and why. However, they generally fail to establish causal relationships by answering the 'why' aspect. Therefore, although a questionnaire is an effective method for the gathering of facts, it can only really test a

r

hypothesis or add weight to a theory, rather than providing 'proof'. With this type of research, 'proof' will be a social construct anyway, as it will be based upon the perceptions, opinions and beliefs of those involved. Designing effective questionnaires is difficult. The research question and who the questionnaire is for will dictate the questions that will go on it. To avoid bias, questions that 'lead' the person filling it in towards a specific answer must be guarded against. Asking pupils 'When did you start taking part in extra-curricular activities?' assumes that a child has actually taken part. It can also be dangerous to assume knowledge on behalf of the respondent as if they fail to understand the question, the information which they feedback may be unreliable. By using closed questions in the questionnaire, the responses may not be perceptive, as these may require the recipient to offer an answer that is not really 'fit for purpose', and fails to allow for the response to be expanded upon to give perceptions or opinions. The use of Likert Scales may counteract this, as they allow the respondent to rate or display their level of response to the question on a scale. These enable the researcher to gain the levels of intensity the questionnaire recipients feel about a particular issue outlined in the question. The researcher needs to take into account that an 'open' questionnaire takes time to complete, and that there will be additional difficulties with the data analysis, as it will prove time-consuming to examine and code all the responses. Coding involves assigning qualitative data that fall into similar categories (themes) with a code. These can be analysed by a number of software programmes, or by the researcher themselves. The analysis can then draw relationships between the coded data. The rate of returns from a closed questionnaire may well be low, especially if there is apathy among the subjects concerning the need to both think and write. Time needs to be spent adequately structuring the questionnaire, and a pilot to a small group of the respondents may help to devise an appropriate structure.

Since there are difficulties in answering 'why' questions through the use of questionnaires, interviews with what Wellington (2000) calls 'key informants' may be a more suitable way of doing this. Interviews are a good means of getting perceptions, opinions and ideals as interviewees can respond by saying what they are thinking. A consideration here which undergraduates need to take into account is the ethical difficulty involved in obtaining permission for children to participate in one-to-one interviews. A focus group involving a small number of relevant students is a way of overcoming ethical issues.

Interviews usually follow one of three different formats, as follows:

1 **Structured:** these suggest little deviation from the set questions, and although they may be easier to analyse, they will rarely fulfil more than what a questionnaire would have done in the first place. It may be possible for the researcher to take the interviewee's body language into account as facial expression and gesture may indicate whether the interviewee has more to say, or stronger feelings than the set questions allow.

2 **Unstructured:** these allow the interviewee the opportunity to take the lead as there is little set pattern to the questioning. The interview may deviate away from the research questions, and although it may provide useful additional information, the data provided may struggle to cover the intended areas of study. It may also provide a large amount of (often unnecessary) information.

3 **Semi-structured:** this is the type of questioning that students involved in social research most commonly use. The procedure is not only to follow a set list of questions, but also to allow for the interviewer to respond towards the answers that the interviewee provides. This may not only result in useful additional information, but also allow the interviewer to keep the interview more focused upon the research questions. However, factors such as bias or probing questions need to be taken into account when responding to the interviewee's answers.

Time and location need to be taken into consideration when conducting interviews. Aspects such as allowing the interviewee time to shape their responses without being interrupted, privacy to ensure that the interview schedule is not disturbed, and that it takes place in an environment where the interviewee feels comfortable will contribute to its success. There are other considerations such as whether to take notes, or to make an audio recording, with both positive and negative arguments for both approaches. By taking notes, it will be difficult to get a verbatim transcription, and useful data may be lost. However, transcription can be a lengthy, time-consuming part of the data collection, and recording the interview may fail to pick up on aspects of the interviewee's body language. The verbatim transcription should be approved by the interviewee before it is used in case there is information given that they want to discount. All aspects of interviews should be negotiated with the interviewees in advance.

The nature of how the questionnaires and interviews are structured should reflect upon the methodological approach undertaken with the

r

research. By identifying the types of interview and questionnaire as ranging from structured to unstructured, and from closed to open, it is possible to see the relationships between the paradigms of positivism and interpretivism. The structured, closed-type questions are more positivistic, while the open, less structured questions will be linked with an interpretivist approach. This knowledge should aid the researcher with the construction of their epistemological starting point.

The researcher can also gather data through observations. This can range from being completely involved as a participant to taking on the role of an uninvolved observer. The interpretivist would claim that even observing would constitute involvement. The aspects being observed will dictate the methods of observation to be used (Sparkes, 2002). A positivistic approach would look to structure the observation and enable the researcher to record specific behaviours or traits and quantify them. The interpretivist observer would look at the circumstances surrounding the observable behaviours and take these into consideration during the analysis. A structure would still be required for the observations to ensure that the focus of the research question(s) wasn't lost. The observer undertaking an overt or a covert role during the data collection process needs to be considered, as the behaviours of those involved in the research process may change if they are aware that they are being observed. Within a PESS setting observation has the potential to be a most useful form of research but it is vital that informed consent (*see separate entry*) must be secured before the investigation can begin. The issues here will surround those of safeguarding children along with maintaining the trust of teachers anxious to discover how any data collected will be subsequently reported. It makes the notion of voluntary informed consent extremely important.

See also: *Epistemology/Ontology, Ethics, Informed Consent, Methodology, Reliability/Validity, Research Approach*

FURTHER READING

Curtner-Smith, M., 'Methodological Issues in Research' in Laker, A., ed., *The Sociology of Sport and Physical Education* (Routledge, 2002), pp. 36–57

Sparkes, A., 'The Paradigms Debate: An Extended Review and a Celebration of Difference' in Sparkes, A., ed., *Research in Physical Education and Sport* (Falmer 1992), pp. 9–60

RISK ASSESSMENT/MANAGEMENT

Physical activities by their very nature involve elements of challenge and risk and it is the necessary exposure to these elements that facilitate and indeed enhance learning in PE. Each activity, however, will involve a different level of risk and therefore the potential to cause harm and injury to students. It is the teacher of PE who has the professional responsibility to ensure that the risks of the teaching space and the activity being undertaken are managed so that they are appropriate for the age and the physical, developmental and emotional capabilities of the individual students being taught. Through this process, the aim is to reduce the potential for injury without necessarily detracting from the benefits of the activity. Where the activity involves high risk (such as certain outdoor adventurous activities and contact sports) then there is obviously a necessarily higher level of awareness and risk management to be considered. This will almost certainly include having to refer to school, local authority or national governing body (or other) recommendations and requirements as part of the required process. Risk management in PE provides 'a well-managed and safe educational context', establishing 'common and well-understood codes of practice', providing 'consistent administrative and organisational procedures' and ensuring that 'statutory and local requirements are understood and complied with' (AfPE, 2008).

There are several principles that should underpin effective risk management in PE. The basis of this is to consider the activity or event from three perspectives. These are the *people* involved in the activity, the *context* in which the activity takes place and the *organisation* of the activity (AfPE, 2008). There are five steps to assessing risk:

1 Identifying the hazard.
2 Deciding who might be harmed and how.
3 Evaluating the risks and deciding on precautions.
4 Recording findings and implementing them.
5 Reviewing assessment; updating it if necessary (HSE, 2006, p. 2).

Written risk assessments should be carried out and updated regularly. Recommended risk assessment formats for PESS, based on the principles outlined above, can be found in the recent version of *Safe Practice in Physical Education and School Sport* (AfPE, 2008). Risk assessment will include consideration of locations such as changing and showering spaces, PE equipment stores, and indoor and outdoor teaching spaces, in

r

addition to the various activities themselves. Extensive risk assessments should also be undertaken for offsite education and educational trips. In addition to teaching 'safely' by managing risk effectively, teachers should also educate their students to assess risk by teaching 'safety'. The National Curriculum (QCA, 2008) outlines this through the 'General Aims', developing confident individuals who 'take managed risks and stay safe'. The 'Key Concepts' for PE include the ability to 'recognise hazards and make decisions about how to control any risks to themselves and others'. It is therefore essential that a well-designed PE curriculum should also ensure elements of safety education for students across a variety of contexts in order to develop a lifelong awareness of risk and its management.

See also: *Safety Education*

FURTHER READING

Association for Physical Education (AfPE), *Safe Practice in Physical Education and School Sport* (Coachwise, 2008)

Health and Safety Executive (HSE), *Five Steps to Risk Assessment* (HSE Books, 2006)

Severs, J. with Whitlam, P. & Woodhouse, J., *Safety and Risk in Primary School Physical Education* (Routledge, 2003)

S

SAFEGUARDING

The development of PESS initiatives nationally in recent years has meant that teachers are always seeking to provide innovative ways of ensuring a high quality of experience for pupils within this setting. This will often involve the recruitment of new staff, adults other than teachers (AOTTS), adoption of new teaching strategies and activities, the development of partnerships with clubs and other community organisations and of course coaches. These initiatives, along with the general professional expectations placed upon teachers, bring with them necessary concerns regarding the safeguarding of pupils, the major concern of which is to ensure that children are not placed in the way of risk or harm when under the supervision of professionals and volunteer staff. All such people working in PESS need to be clear about their duty of care to children and young people, understanding fully the expected and acceptable behaviours associated with the role undertaken. Thorough checks on individuals are undertaken when all new teaching staff are appointed to schools to ensure that they are appropriately qualified to work with children and young people.

When working with partners in/from the community, clear safeguarding protocols need to be established so that each person is fully aware of the expectations placed upon them in protecting children in their charge from coming to harm. Schools must be fully satisfied that all adults working with children have undertaken the relevant Criminal Records Bureau (CRB) and Independent Safeguarding Authority (ISA) checks, that they hold the necessary level of qualifications, that they are recognised by their NGB and that they come with appropriate references. A thorough induction into the school/departmental procedures and expectations needs to take place. Each school will have a designated safeguarding/child protection coordinator and will have relevant policies and codes of practice in conjunction with the local authority. The teacher of PE will have many additional considerations with regards to safeguarding children. These include:

- Supervision of changing.
- Supervision of young leaders working with children.
- Appropriate qualifications and induction/supervision of coaches in PESS.
- The ability to identify potential indicators of abuse and a clear understanding of the recommended local procedures for reporting them.
- Expected recommendations and conduct in terms of physical contact with pupils; for example, when supporting children in a gymnastic skill.
- Relevant policies are in place and adhered to regarding the procedures for extra-curricular PE, offsite fixtures, trips and visits including parental consent, parental information, risk assessment, supervision and transport.
- Policies are in place and adhered to regarding digital imagery, filming and use of the internet for the purposes of PESS. It is important that any whole-school policy confirms this.

It is clear that a great deal of care and planning is required to ensure that children and young people are safe in PESS. One of the skills of the teacher is to ensure that this takes place without deterring the pupils from having an enjoyable, meaningful learning experience.

FURTHER READING

Association for Physical Education (AfPE), *Safe Practice in Physical Education and School Sport* (Coachwise, 2008)

Baginsky, M., ed., *Safeguarding Children in Schools* (JKP, 2008)

Spencer, K., 'Safeguarding', *Physical Education Matters,* 4 (1) (2009), pp. 39–40

Spencer, K., 'Safeguarding Children and Young People', *Physical Education Matters,* 3 (3) (2008), pp. 12–14

SAFETY EDUCATION

For many years PE teachers have tended to focus purely on the safe delivery of lessons through considering their own practice. The modern physical educationalist needs to consider not only the teaching of activities safely but the teaching of 'safety' itself (ROSPA, 2007). This involves informing and engaging pupils in the process of taking responsibility for their own safety, health and well-being and understanding the possible consequences of their actions or that of others' actions. Where both teachers and pupils understand their responsibilities towards fostering a safe working environment, then the levels of risk are minimised.

An element of safety education underpins many of the health and personal safeguarding policies and developments in (physical) education in recent years. The National Curriculum (QCA, 1999) included a statutory 'General Teaching requirement for Health and Safety' which applied to PE. This was drawn up jointly between the Qualifications and Assessment Authority (QCA) and the Health and Safety Executive (HSE). This guidance included a requirement that teachers teach pupils about recognising hazards, assessing and controlling risks and managing their environment to ensure health and safety. Further to this there were subject-specific expectations contained within the programmes of study. Under the revised National Curriculum (QCA, 2007), one of the aims is to develop 'confident individuals who are able to live safe and fulfilling lives' and who can 'take managed risks and stay safe' (QCA, 2007, p. 189). In the Physical Education Programme of Study, there are key references to safety awareness for pupils. For example, Key Concept 1.4(b) 'Healthy and Active Lifestyles' recommends pupils should recognise physical activity which is 'safe and enjoyable' (QCA, 2007, p. 191), and Key Process 2.2(d) 'Making and Applying Decisions' clearly outlines that pupils should 'recognise hazards and make decisions about how to control any risks to themselves and others' (QCA, 2007, p. 192). Within the 'Range and Content' section, reference is made to overcoming 'challenges of

S

171

an adventurous nature as in life-saving and personal survival in swimming and outdoor activities' and also 'exercising safely and effectively' (QCA, 2007, p. 194). The DfES (2001) in 'Safety Education: Guidance for Schools' suggests that safety education can encourage young people to take part 'confidently and competently' and to take 'decisions and actions' (2001, p. 8). The document also recommends that pupils should be taught to recognise hazards, assess risk and control risk. 'Every Child Matters: Change for Children' (DfES, 2004) also has as one of its outcomes 'Stay safe', and ROSPA/DCSF/PSHE Association (2008) provide a summary of evidence from research recommending ten basic principles for effective safety education teaching as a whole-school approach:

1 Encourage the adoption of, or reinforce, a whole-school approach, within the wider community.
2 Use active approaches to teaching and learning (including interactive and experiential learning).
3 Involve young people in real decisions to help them stay safe.
4 Assess children and young people's learning needs.
5 Teach safety as part of a comprehensive personal social and health curriculum.
6 Use realistic and relevant settings and resources.
7 Work in partnership.
8 Address known risk and protective factors.
9 Address psychosocial aspects of safety, e.g. confidence, resilience, self-esteem, self-efficacy.
10 Adopt positive approaches that model and reward safe behaviour, within a safe, supportive environment.

After some of the high-profile legal cases involving school pupils on trips, visits and offsite activities in recent years, consideration should be given to ensuring pupils are aware of the expectations and safety implications placed upon them. The DfEE advises that where pupils are involved in the planning of such activities, then they will tend to make 'more informed decisions and will be less at risk' (1998, p. 16). Within the 'Learning Outside the Classroom' document (DfES, 2006) it is highlighted through the outcomes that the educational values of such activities include developing 'the ability to deal with uncertainty' and 'provide challenge and the opportunity to take acceptable levels of risk' (p. 3). AfPE highlights the importance of safety education for pupils through *Safe Practice in Physical Education and School Sport* (AfPE, 2008). Each section contains valuable outlines of 'what pupils should know', as it recognises the importance of involving pupils in 'the assessment and management of risk at a level appropriate to their age, ability, experience and behaviour' (p. 3). For example, within the 'General and Common Principles' chapter it emphasises the importance of pupils recognising how to participate appropriately within the activity, to respect the decisions of officials, to manage risk and to be attired correctly for the activity undertaken.

Effective safety education through the PE programme can provide immediate and long-term benefits in educating pupils to consider their own safety and that of those around them. Knowledge and understanding of, for example, the assessment and management of risk, and safe lifting, carrying and lowering techniques can impact on the everyday lives of pupils beyond their compulsory schooling. Physical education teachers can instil an understanding of lifting, carrying and lowering apparatus such as benches and mats, awareness of rules and regulations and how to respect the decisions of those in authority such as sports officials and leaders. By developing in pupils an awareness of their own behaviour and its impact on others and by encouraging them to dress correctly for physical activity teachers can instil a basic safety appreciation with lessons for life.

FURTHER READING
Association for Physical Education (AfPE), *Safe Practice in Physical Education and School Sport* (Coachwise, 2008)

SCHOOL SPORT AMBASSADORS

Olympians and Paralympians appointed by the YST and part funded by commercial sponsorship. A total of six sporting celebrities such as Darren Campbell and Denise Lewis can be contacted through the YST (*see separate entry*) to visit schools and school sporting events across the United Kingdom with the objective of encouraging more children to take part in PESS. A visit by a school sport ambassador can involve opportunities to speak in assemblies, contribute to a PE lesson or even coincide with a sports day. There is a direct link with YST targets to support the development of competitors, coaches, leaders, volunteers and officials. This initiative follows on from the appointment of Dame Kelly Holmes in 2006 as National School Sport Champion, who over a two-year period met with pupils and teachers around the country with the aim of developing more interest in PE and school sport. More specific targets included support for finding and nurturing young sporting talent alongside a desire to encourage more participation from teenage girls.

See also: *National School Sport Week*

FURTHER READING
www.youthsporttrust.org

SCHOOL SPORTS COLLEGES (SSCS)

Specialist school colleges aiming to act as beacons of excellence within a national school sport structure. The first was opened in 1996 and the target is for 400 in total. SSCs are at the hub of School Sport Partnerships (SSPs), whereby the specialist college works within a family of usually eight secondary schools who in turn develop links with feeder primary schools. Each SSP receives approximately £270,000 per year from which a partnership development manager (PDM) is appointed along with school sports coordinators (SSCOs) and primary link teachers (PLTs). The aims and objectives of SSCOs are to promote PESS at all levels whether it is to increase participation or to meet the needs of elite youth sport.

For a school to achieve SSC status they will need to have already achieved Sportsmark (*see Activemark*) status, which needs to be upgraded to Sportsmark Gold after three years for successful re-designation of specialism. The school will also need to demonstrate willingness to improve sports facilities, have a good school sport reputation and provide evidence for availability of sponsorship funds. All this will need to be incorporated into a three-year development plan. The location of existing SSCs makes for an interesting study. Houlihan (in Bailey & Kirk, eds., 2009) has noted the preponderance of many of the first SSCs to be located in communities of socio-economic disadvantage. This coincides with New Labour policy concerning the regeneration of communities through multi-agency partnerships; for example, between health and education (*see Government and Policy*).

The effectiveness and impact to date within SSCs suggests that more high quality PE and sport is taking place (Ofsted, 2004; Loughborough

Partnership, 2005; Houlihan in Bailey & Kirk, eds., 2009). The profile of the subject has been raised, there is a wider range of opportunities at both curricular and extra-curricular level and more CPD is available. Ofsted (2009) inspected twelve SSCs, nine of which were deemed to be good or outstanding in 'overall effectiveness'. Interestingly, the same report suggested that the impact on areas of the curriculum other than PE was less tangible, which may support a finding by Houlihan (in Bailey & Kirk, eds., 2009) who felt that there was some early resistance towards the concept of SSCs from other subjects. Green (2008) believes that effective research on SSCs to date is limited, although the effects on improvements in primary school PE are acknowledged. Furthermore, evidence to support success in reaching specific target groups is mixed (Loughborough Partnership, 2005 & 2009).

By appointing a sports college to oversee a family of schools, a two-tier system has been created whereby at a local level it is now effectively one school that has control over both budgetary and policy concerns. Tensions within the objectives of SSCs focus on a possible conflict between aims for participation and community involvement as opposed to elite development. Furthermore, any vocational aspirations for pupils as espoused by other subject specialist colleges are tempered by what are perceived to be a lack of opportunities for gainful employment within the leisure industry (Houlihan in Bailey & Kirk, eds., 2009). There are also possibilities for contested areas between PE teachers and the increasing use of external providers such as coaches who may operate from a different agenda. In fact, Houlihan (ibid.) suggests that although some PE teachers feel reinvigorated by the whole SSC concept, do they really exert much influence over policy? There is a feeling that NGBs are starting to get a foothold within the curriculum and that senior management teams are deciding on priority sports alongside using SSC status for publicity. King's localised study of SSPs (2009) observes the effectiveness of partnerships within the regeneration of disadvantaged neighbourhoods. Here, SSPs have contributed towards improved exam results for young people and increased leisure opportunities for the local population. However, although largely successful in terms of participation and pupil engagement, tensions exist: first, with the existence of so many disparate interest groups; and second, with the local authority whose objectives differ from those of a national school sports strategy. Relationships with primary schools are largely good but struggle within the provision of after school activities and links with

S

community clubs are hindered by the fact that SSCs are not built with dual use in mind. There is also a feeling that the voluntary sector has been pushed to one side in a policy area now controlled by professionals.

In sum, there is little doubt that SSCs have helped with community regeneration. However, the development of elite performers will always be problematic within a national sports culture that is increasingly failing to recognise the importance of school sport; in fact some NGBs now withdraw pupils from the whole process and perhaps just look upon PESS as a fallback for undiscovered talent. A good example of this is the Football Association, with their decision to assume responsibility for the national under-16 boys' team rather than leave it to the schools to organise. The setting up of academies run by professional football clubs follows a similar vein. So, if SSCs could focus on a main objective to increase levels of physical activity in young people then maybe the rationale for their existence could become clearer.

See also: *Partnership Development Manager (PDM), Physical Education and Sport Strategy for Young People (PESSYP), School Sports Coordinator (SSCO)*

FURTHER READING

Houlihan, B., 'Sporting Excellence, School and Sports Development: The Politics of Crowded Policy Spaces' in Bailey, R. & Kirk, D., eds., *The Routledge Physical Education Reader* (Routledge, 2009), pp. 61–81

King, N., *Sport Policy and Governance: Local Perspectives* (Elsevier, 2009)

SCHOOL SPORTS COORDINATOR (SSCO)

A school sports coordinator (SSCO) is a key policy actor within the infrastructure of the School Sport Partnership (SSP). A typical SSP includes a PDM, SSCOs and PLTs. Each SSP will have one PDM; however, the number of SSCOs and PLTs will vary depending upon the number of schools within the SSP. SSCOs are based within secondary schools and are responsible for the development of high quality PE within designated curriculum time and beyond, particularly in the forging of links with feeder primary schools. They aim to build upon the opportunities for individuals to engage in high quality PE by providing and improving chances to partake in school sport, including inter- and intra-school competitions. SSCOs ultimately aim to develop out-of-school-hours learning, often through improved development of club links. Many SSCOs are existing secondary school PE teachers who have taken on the extra responsibility within two key settings. Thus, a 'typical' week for an SSCO can consist of two days dedicated to the role and a further three days teaching PE. SSCOs liaise with the PDM, who is 'normally' based within the SSP sports college, and the PLTs, who are based within the feeder primary schools. The SSCO is imperative in improving the overall provision of high quality PESS through transition phases across each key stage.

The Loughborough Partnership (2008) found that two-thirds of SSCOs are female. Given the fact that SSPs have taken time for policies to embed and mature, the same source has found that the SSCO work-force is relatively stable, maturing and gaining in experience since the last report in 2004. Ninety-eight per cent of SSCOs have qualified teacher status and it will be interesting to see if this trend will change with future appointments.

See also: *High Quality Physical Education, Public Service Agreement (PSA)*

FURTHER READING:
www.youthsporttrust.org

SELF-ESTEEM

This refers to the value placed on the self and is often used interchangeably with the term self-concept. For physical educationists, adherence to Fox's physical self-perception model (in Biddle & Mutrie, 2008) may be useful as a rationale for physical activity programmes. With its emphasis on the sub-domains of sport competence, body attractiveness, perceived strength and physical condition this model suggests that how a person views him/herself physically will influence how they feel generally. Usually, then, self-esteem is commonly seen as the most important indicator of psychological well-being.

The evidence that the psychological well-being of adolescents can be improved through exercise, particularly for those participants who are low in self-esteem, is substantial (Fox in Biddle et al., eds., 2000). Here, physical

S

fitness and aerobics have produced better results than skill- and sport-based programmes. This is due to the fact that these are less competitive activities with little need for the acquisition of skills. Moreover, activities and locations which involve self or group choice also produce stronger effects. These positive findings are a salutary reminder that PE programmes have the potential to do the opposite as they are largely compulsory and offer little scope for personal choice (ibid.).

There are two research approaches to self-esteem and exercise. The first suggests that it acts as a motivational determinant for physical activity with the suggestion that participants high in self-esteem are more likely to engage in exercise as it is an area to enhance or maintain self-worth. The second approach is the 'skill development hypothesis' (Sonstroem in Biddle & Mutrie, 2008). This advocates that self-esteem can be changed through physical activity by the development of both skills and task mastery. Biddle (ibid.) stresses that the two hypotheses are in fact inter-related, in that participants often gain initial self-esteem at the start of exercise programmes and so develop motivation to progress towards further engagement.

Self-esteem can be linked to a mental health problem that is on the increase in England even among children – one in five young people are reckoned to suffer from a related experience during the course of a year. The most common psychiatric disorder is depression and there is evidence of a developing trend, particularly in socially disadvantaged areas (Rutter & Smith in Biddle et al., eds., 2000). The seriousness of this problem is further compounded by the suggestion that there may be a link between childhood depression and gains in weight and obesity later on in adult life (Hasler in Biddle & Mutrie, 2008). The role of physical activity in ameliorating this problem is one of growing interest for health care professionals. At the moment existing research suggests that participation in sport, physical education and general activity can lead to psychological well-being, which is the state of contentment, satisfaction, peace and happiness (Biddle & Mutrie, 2008). The relationship between physical activity and mental health warrants further investigation with findings that could have an informed impact on future PE programmes.

FURTHER READING
Biddle, S. & Mutrie, N., *Psychology of Physical Activity* (2nd edn, Routledge, 2008)

Biddle, S., Fox, K. & Boutcher, S., eds., *Physical Activity and Psychological Well-Being* (Routledge, 2000)

SPORTS DEVELOPMENT OFFICERS (SDOS)

These are community coaches used to supplement a school's PESS programme. SDOs are symptomatic of how PE and sport professionals are now required to work alongside each other in partnerships as part of a performance-driven culture aiming to develop physical activity for young people. They are usually employed by local authorities either in a sports-specific role or as multi-activity leaders. Those who take on the former role have been instrumental in organising some of the better school sport opportunities in recent years; the Rugby Union Emerging Schools Competitions, for instance. This latter tournament is an excellent example of an NGB encouraging more schools to play sport by arranging the correct level of competition for beginners. It relies heavily on collaboration between rugby development officers and local school teachers, offering schools the chance to progress from regional tournaments to a national final at Twickenham.

Sport development as a concept faces a possible crisis of identity and direction. There are undoubtedly tensions between the quest for *elite* sport development and the need for action at the participation level. Consequently, there are disagreements between the policy makers as to where the focus should be (Lyle in Hylton & Bramham, eds., 2008). Any attempts to place sport development in the middle of a continuum between elite and participation levels can only create further confusion. This can present an awkward relationship with the coaching process as well (ibid.). Is the SDO concerned with retention of participants or pursuing excellence? Is the quest for development or for talent identification?

It is this perceived relationship with coaching that can conflict with sport development's involvement in PE programmes. Thus, Lyle (ibid.) suggests that sports coaching has traditionally neglected the delivery of pedagogical skills and is less suitable for school-based settings. Here, concerns for technical development and competition preparation contrast with a beginner's needs, who may look upon sport as a means of achieving other benefits. In fact, the entrance of SDOs into the PESS setting is another contribution towards 'a crowded policy arena' (Houlihan, 2000). As a result the differing philosophies between teachers, SDOs and coaches

179

can create tensions, particularly when the first of these professions believe that their job has become de-skilled with possible replacement by the latter two occupations. Green (2008) attributes the involvement of SDOs to increased class sizes in the 1990s when teachers started to look out into the community for help. This gave the impression of legitimising the practice of using unqualified teachers. This also comes back to the central concern that PE is involving itself with too many external agencies and thus is leading to a shift in the balance of power within the PE community.

Will SDOs and community coaches take over in the future? Will PE teachers be 'relegated' to the role of overseeing exams while others are left to train pupils in specific sports? Every step should be taken to avoid the 'de-professionalisation' of PE by upholding the status of those specialists trained to teach the subject. What has become apparent is that in the quest to elevate the status of the subject too many outside interests have been allowed to gain a foothold, making PE a battleground for influence – and not necessarily in the best interests of the children.

FURTHER READING
Hylton, K. & Bramham, P., eds., *Sports Development: Policy, Process and Practice* (2nd edn, Routledge, 2008)

SPORT EDUCATION
A thematic approach towards teaching PE based on seasons, formal competitions, keeping records and festivity. It represents a conceptual approach to teaching and is there as a voluntary model for schools to follow. Developed in the early 1990s at Ohio State University, the programme started from an initial perception that PE lessons were too reliant on the teaching of skills in isolation rather than in game situations. It is based on the supposition that the practices and rituals of sport are not addressed in schools, particularly the roles and responsibilities of team membership (Siedentop et al., 1994).

Sport Education involves seasons of play, which can run across terms or throughout the school year culminating in an end competition or festival. Teams are selected to stay constant throughout with students taking on various roles, which can vary from that of captain to a journalist who is expected to make a written account of how the match has gone. Records and statistics are kept to both stimulate interest and inform future practice. A key objective is to promote enjoyment in PE lessons through the celebration of sport; for example, classes should be given the opportunity to design kits with their own logos and assume the names of national teams. Sport Education aims to develop students' physical, cognitive and affective skills by avoiding any of the negativity that surrounds modern sport. Initially it was promoted within the context of games with other areas of activity somewhat unexplored. Development has taken place mainly within secondary schools rather than in primary education, although the latter could be a prime context considering the potential that Sport Education has for cross-curricular themes such as in science, English and geography. Research to date has highlighted the success of Sport Education in stimulating interest both for lower ability children (Carlson in Penny et al., eds., 2005) and for previously disaffected girls who have enjoyed the less formal and didactic style used by the teacher involved (Hastie in Penny et al., eds., 2005). There is still a need for research to be undertaken into effects on more able performers, particularly within the aspect of skill acquisition. Here, concern has been expressed over the lack of prominence given to effective instruction for this very purpose.

Sport Education is now firmly established within the USA, Australia and New Zealand. It is less popular within the United Kingdom, which is somewhat surprising given recent attempts to link PESS together alongside government objectives for combating health disorders and reducing crime (Penny et al., eds., 2005). A possible way forward here could be to promote Sport Education more fully within ITE programmes.

FURTHER READING

Penny, D., Clarke, G., Quill, M. & Kinchin, G., eds., *Sport Education in Physical Education* (Routledge, 2005)

Siedentop, D. Hastie, P. & Van der Mars, H., *Complete Guide to Sport Education* (Human Kinetics, 1994)

S

SPORT ENGLAND

This government-appointed body is a distributor of both exchequer and National Lottery money towards sport at all levels of participation. Sport England function around three main stated outcomes: growing, sustaining and excelling. They work in partnership with UK Sport, which has responsibility for elite success and the YST (*see separate entry*), which aims to develop PESS. In the 1990s Sport England, then known as the English Sports Council, became closely involved with PESS through the 'National Junior Sport Programme' (*see Sport: Raising the Game*) mainly in the role of distributor of funds. However, with the growth of the YST, direct involvement in PESS has diminished.

Today, Sport England are accountable to the Department for Culture, Media and Sport (DCMS). Their closest current involvement with PESS is found as part of PESSYP, where in collaboration with County Sports Partnerships (*see separate entry*) they have substantial input, again as a distributor of finance, to the extra-curricular aspect of this initiative. Through this they aim to encourage participation in a variety of sports volunteering and leadership (*see separate entry*) opportunities; for example, Step Into Sport.

See also: *Youth Sport Trust (YST)*

FURTHER READING
www.sportengland.org

SPORT: RAISING THE GAME
Published by the Department of National Heritage in 1995, this was only the second ever government white paper on sport in the United Kingdom; notable because it reflected the personal endorsement of the then prime minister, John Major. This policy document gave support for the revised National Curriculum, which made games compulsory as an area of activity at KS 4. Ofsted was now required to report on extra-curricular sport and each school would have to publish details of after-hours programmes in their prospectus. Initiatives were put in place to enhance sport in higher education and Ofsted were instructed to inspect Initial Teacher Education (ITE) programmes. Applications were invited for a British Academy of Sport, which eventually became the UK Sports Institute in 1996 administered by UK Sport. Proposals were also outlined for a 'National Junior Sport Programme', which aimed to enhance sport in schools through the following four initiatives:
1 Challenge Club Funding (money to develop school-club links)
2 Sportsmark/Sportsmark Gold (*see Activemark*)
3 Coaching for Teachers (opportunities for teachers to gain NGB awards in school time)

4 School Community Sports Initiative (lottery money for capital projects such as new sports halls)

The statement was unique for the biographical input of the Prime Minister John Major, who was determined to make a start on improving the nation's performance in international sport by giving PESS more prominence in schools. Moreover, it signified the restoration of elitism, heritage and nationalism through PESS, values emphasised by the Major administration in the introductory statement itself.

The reaction from the PE profession was mixed. The privileging of sport over PE and the renewed emphasis on games was a matter of concern for some (Kay, 1998), although Green (2008) reported that it was the latter factor which appealed most to some teachers. Generally, the initiatives involved met with approval, although there was a call for more funding to be made available. The main legacy has been Sportsmark, which initially failed to attract applicants due to the stipulation concerning curriculum time allocation for PE in schools; criteria which failed to acknowledge that most schools were only offering the minimum requirement of two hours a week at Key Stage 3 and one hour at Key Stage 4. Critics suggested that this particular initiative had been hastily put together with too much emphasis on policies and planning rather than on quality in lessons (Spencer, 1998). However, subsequent changes to eligibility criteria eventually resulted in more successful applications from schools. The award is now an essential prerequisite for sports college status with Sportsmark Gold necessary for re-designation after three years.

A more holistic critical analysis suggests that the document conveniently omitted previous principles surrounding sports policy such as 'Sport for All' and, probably due to Conservative suspicion of devolved power, ignored the importance of local authorities (Houlihan in Bailey & Kirk, eds., 2009). Houlihan (ibid.) also believes that the statement diminished the sports continuum of foundation, participation, performance and excellence. Thus the emphasis on school sport as a means of achieving excellence undermined the contributions previously made at foundation and participation level, so leading to a linear view of sports development.

However, purely from a PE viewpoint, it is fair to say that any reservations concerning language and terminology used in 'Sport: Raising the Game' were relatively minor compared to the realisation that for once a prominent politician appeared to care. Alongside an availability of lottery money introduced earlier the same year prospects for the future of school sport in particular began to change for the better.

FURTHER READING

Spencer, K., 'Sportsmark: A Personal Viewpoint', *British Journal of Physical Education,* Autumn (1998), pp. 31–33

SPORTSMARK

see Activemark

SPORTS PARTNERSHIP MARK

see Activemark

SUBJECT ASSOCIATIONS (PE)

A student of PE will work in an environment among like-minded people with a common interest and enthusiasm for their subject area. Once full teacher status has been achieved there are opportunities to be part of a local association for PE teachers, sharing ideas and views on topics related to the subject. There may well be local groups set up for this networking. In particular, there are opportunities to join a subject association which might be at a county, regional, national or even international level. Some of these have student membership categories. Subject associations act as representative bodies promoting their subject area, providing relevant and specific CPD opportunities and keeping their membership up to date with new developments in teaching and learning. Subject associations will have web-based resources, which may include the information just described. They may also produce relevant resources for download or purchase, professional journals and information about conferences. Some may also be able to provide insurance. PE subject associations include:

- **The Association for Physical Education (AfPE):** UK representative organisation for people and agencies delivering or supporting the delivery of PE in schools and in the wider community.
- **European Physical Education Association (EUPEA):** An

umbrella organisation of European physical education associations. It was founded in 1991 to promote PE all over Europe.

- **The International Association of Physical Education and Sport for Girls and Women (IAPESGW):** An organisation with a primary aim to support and bring together interested professionals from around the world who are working in the fields of PE, dance and sport.
- **National Dance Teachers Association (NDTA):** A subject association for dance in schools and a membership organisation for teachers and dance education professionals.
- **North Western Counties Physical Education Association (NWCPEA):** An organisation dedicated to areas of school PE in the north-west of England since 1925.

Information on the organisations and their contribution to PE can be found on their individual websites. It must be stressed that this is only a representative sample of associations for illustration.

FURTHER READING
See the websites of the various organisations above.

S

TEACHING STRATEGY

The choice and range of teaching methods used for a lesson. It is the term used to describe the manner in which a learning experience is conducted – a combination of teacher interpretation and the methods employed. This differs from a teaching style, which is the teacher behaviour used to achieve learning objectives; for example, communication, rewards and personal effort. Mawer (1999) suggests that 'styles', 'strategies' and 'approaches' are all terms used interchangeably, although he has a preference for the latter as this is used in NCPE (1992). In fact, Green (2008) is of the opinion that the differing terminology has created confusion; he has a preference for the term 'teaching styles'.

There has been considerable government encouragement for teachers to employ a range of teaching strategies (DfEE, 1992, 1995) and developing a repertoire of teaching styles has become a necessary part of professional development. At the same time there has also been a call for more pupil-centred and less direct teaching approaches (Whitehead & Capel, 1993; Ofsted, 1995). The factors involved in the selection of a teaching strategy are complex and do not exist in isolation. Decisions made here should bear in mind both the learning objectives and learning outcomes, be mindful of the learner and take a realistic view of the teaching context. For teaching styles in particular the spectrum devised by Mosston & Ashworth (1986), varying from the teacher-centred command style to the more open discovery approach, is an extremely useful guide for PE teachers.

There is considerable evidence to suggest that many teachers, particularly when teaching boys in PE lessons, employ a narrow range of teaching approaches mainly based on the command-style approach (Mawer, 1999). This revelation has perhaps resulted from the inception of NCPE in 1992, where the statutory requirements for assessment exposed a predominantly male reliance on direct teaching styles. However, research on the effectiveness of various styles and strategies is unequivocal (Sicilia-Camacho & Brown, 2008). What has become clear, though, is that each teaching context can differ markedly from the next and teachers should be open to developing a number of approaches, all of which are potentially interchangeable in the one lesson. A good example of this would be a gymnastics lesson which starts with a command style as the teacher states aims and objectives then moves on to the practice style while pupils actually do the tasks set. From there a reciprocal approach is recommended by asking the children to observe each other to highlight faults and corrections. The lesson could then progress to the guided discovery style in the form of an instructional teaching card for the pupils to learn a new skill from. Unfortunately, though, there is considerable scepticism that this is the case, based on a feeling that many teachers adhere to what has worked in the past and have become increasingly less receptive to change (Macfadyen & Bailey, 2002). Once again the ITE setting becomes crucial for future teachers to be made aware of new, innovative approaches towards the teaching of PESS.

FURTHER READING

Capel, S., Leask, M. & Turner, T., eds., *Learning to Teach in the Secondary School* (3rd edn, RoutledgeFalmer, 2003)

Hardy, C.A. & Mawer, M., eds., *Learning and Teaching in Physical Education* (RoutledgeFalmer, 1999)

TRAINING (FITNESS)

Training involves undertaking activities that will maintain or improve an individual's performance in sport and physical activity. It is important that training is carefully planned and that the long- and short-term performance objectives are clearly identified and understood; also, that appropriate strategies, techniques and training methods are used that will help the individual to achieve those objectives and, where relevant, peak at the required point in the programme (*see Periodisation*). In modern-day training, the performer and the coach/teacher, must have a sound understanding of the underpinning principles to ensure that training is effective in developing performance. For many sports, this may necessarily involve a good understanding of energy transfer within the activity and the selection of appropriate training methods to improve energy delivery and utilisation (McArdle et al., 2000).

There are a wide variety of different training methods and techniques designed to improve specific aspects of fitness; some are outlined below. If training is to be successful, however, it must follow a set of principles irrespective of the method(s) selected. These 'principles of training' include specificity, progressive overload, reversibility and individual differences. The principle of *specificity* refers to the need to ensure that specific methods are required in order to achieve specific desired effects and adaptations. *Progressive overload* involves working the body harder than it is accustomed to. Adjusting the frequency, intensity or duration of training in a controlled way can have the desired effect. *Reversibility* or 'detraining' occurs over a period of time once the individual stops training and the benefits originally gained are gradually lost. In terms of *individual differences*, it must be remembered that individuals will react to training in different ways and they will have varying starting points at the commencement of a training programme. This needs to be considered particularly in the development of individuals within a team activity.

Training methods include variations of interval training where periods of work are interspersed with periods of recovery. The variables that can be adjusted in interval training to ensure appropriate 'overload' include the intensity of the exercise, duration of the exercise, duration of recovery and repetitions of exercise and recovery (McArdle et al., 2000). This is the case in circuit training, for example. Other types of training include weight training, plyometrics (jumping and bounding exercises using the stretch-recoil properties of muscle), pulley work, medicine ball training, and parachute or sled pulling. Endurance training might involve long, slow

distance training, fartlek (varying speed and distances) and other variations of interval training. To develop flexibility, active, static and passive
stretching routines may be used. Within these training methods, selection of correct exercises and correct intensities are important in ensuring
the desired effect (*see Fitness*). The potential for over-training also exists,
where there can be a reduction in the potential to improve and possibly
even result in a 'breakdown in the adaptation process, eventually reducing
performance' (Wilmore & Costill, 2004, p. 376)

FURTHER READING
Wilmore, J.H. & Costill, D.L., *Physiology of Sport and Exercise* (Human
Kinetics, 2004)

TRIPARTITE EDUCATION
A selective policy for secondary school education followed from 1945
onwards and still used by some local authorities (33 LAs out of 149 in
2002). Although implemented alongside the 1944 Butler Education Act
the policy itself was separate to legislation that saw the introduction of a
Minister of Education, the formation of local education authorities and
an attempt to establish a compulsory daily act of worship in all schools.
The tripartite system of education meant that primary school children
would take the '11+' test. A pass resulted in a place at the local grammar
school, while failure would mean attendance at either a secondary modern
or, in some areas, a technical school. Initially introduced as part of the
post-war attempts to work towards a more meritocratic society the policy
became a topic of much political discourse between successive Labour
and Conservative governments. The former felt that grammar schools
soon became the domain of the middle classes and sought a less socially
divisive system. The Conservative Party favoured the process as a means
of promoting individual excellence and achieving standards through
selection. By the 1960s Labour governments had championed a more
inclusive and non-selective comprehensive school ideology, delegating
its implementation at local level. Most authorities did eventually opt for
comprehensive schools, although there are a few areas of the country left
that still retain a selective approach.

PE itself can be seen as part of this post-war social construction of

t

society that impacted upon the types of schools created by the tripartite system (Kirk, 1992). Male PE teachers entered the profession for the first time in some numbers resulting in areas of contestation with their female counterparts. The men were keen to promote games and circuit training, interests gained from a military background; however, this often conflicted with the female teachers' desire to promote more aesthetic activities. This was a time for rebuilding and many schools acquired new playing fields and gyms. The grammar schools in particular were keen to imitate their public school counterparts and so once again a games-playing ideology became pervasive, which in turn was often copied by the secondary modern and technical schools. This contrasted with government attempts to promote a more child-centred approach towards PE as illustrated by the publication of 'Moving and Growing' (1952) and 'Planning the Programme' (1953). These advisory documents stressed the need for creativity and imagination within lessons with each child encouraged to progress at their own rate (Evans & Penny, 2008).

FURTHER READING

Evans, J. & Penny, D., 'Levels on the Playing Field: The Social Construction of Physical Ability in the PE Curriculum', *PE and Sport Pedagogy*, 13 (1) (2008), pp. 31–47

Kirk, D., *Defining Physical Education: The Social Construction of a School Subject in Postwar Britain* (Falmer, 1992)

UK SCHOOL GAMES

This annual multi-sport elite event is for the nation's secondary school students up to 17 years old. In 2006 the first games took place in Glasgow with 1200 children taking part and the aim is for other cities to host in the build-up to 2012. Initial funding involved £1.5 million from the Millennium Commission (superseded by the Big Lottery Fund in 2006) with a further pledge of £6 million for staging the games up to 2011. Local government support is also crucial both for financial support and for the logistics of the event. The full range for sports now extends to athletics, swimming, gymnastics, table tennis, fencing, badminton, hockey, judo and volleyball. Disability sport includes athletics, swimming and table tennis. Staged by the YST, the key themes are:

● To present and encourage talent
● To integrate Olympic and Paralympic themes
● To create opportunities for volunteering
● To advance child protection policies

The selection policy is sport specific and is usually a combination of input from NGBs and school sport governing bodies. Coaches, team managers and other officials are again from the same two sources. Most sports place athletes into nine regional teams for England and one each from Scotland, Wales and Northern Ireland. Progression to the national games through performance trials culminates in an Olympic-style event, with participants staying for four days in a games village. A UK School Games Ambassador has been appointed; in 2010 the Games will take place in the north-east of England.

FURTHER READING

www.ukschoolgames.com

WOLFENDEN REPORT

'Sport and the Community' was published by the Central Council for Physical Recreation (CCPR) in 1960 and chaired by former Head of Uppingham School, Lord Wolfenden; it reported on Britain's future in sport. Written after a period of post-war optimism, the document reflected a realisation that Britain was declining as a world power. The government looked towards sport to counteract this pessimism and act as a unifying force for the nation to come together. The committee chaired by Lord Wolfenden was designed to be small and independent by having no representatives from specific sports. In particular, there was a focus on youth sport as a means of providing talent for future international success. However, according to Kirk (1992) much of the content can also be seen as a method of maintaining social order through games.

The language used within the report paradoxically appeared to represent an apology for public school athleticism while at the same time suggesting that sport and PE could be used to combat juvenile delinquent behaviour. The 'Wolfenden Gap' soon became the accepted expression for the drop-out rate in sports participation among school leavers, particularly in lower socio-economic groups, and has been an area of concern ever since. One of the reasons given for this decline in numbers was the lack

W

of effective links between schools and community sports clubs. This in turn led to the birth of a lobby for a sports policy, ultimately impacting on the call for local councils to provide municipal facilities, which started to appear in the 1970s.

Hargreaves (1986) suggests that although the report was well meaning it can be seen as an agent of social control maintaining the hegemonic structure of society. However, there can be little doubt that games emerged as the dominant discourse from the Wolfenden Committee, particularly as a solution for the nation's disaffected youth. Kirk (1992) also suggests that this games ethic became all-pervasive within the mass secondary schools system created by the tripartite system (*see Tripartite Education*). Generally, the report led to governments getting more involved in sport with the National Playing Fields Association (NPFA) and the CCPR used as forums for political debate. The formation of an Advisory Sports Council in 1965 would soon follow.

See also: *Hegemony, Tripartite Education*

FURTHER READING
Hargreaves, J., *Sport, Power and Culture: A Social and Historical Analysis of Popular Sports in Britain* (Polity Press, 1986)

Kirk, D., *Defining Physical Education: The Social Construction of a School Subject in Postwar Britain* (Falmer, 1992)

YOUNG AMBASSADORS

Introduced in 2006, this programme selects and develops young people as role models to encourage others to get involved in sport leading up to the 2012 Olympics. Each SSP designates two pupils to be ambassadors for two years, the first twelve months to be spent working in the community promoting sport using the Olympic ethos and the second year mentoring the new Young Ambassador intake. One youngster is to be selected as an example of outstanding sporting talent and the other should be chosen purely on the basis of their leadership and volunteering capabilities. The programme is managed by the YST on behalf of the DCSF and the DCMS. Future plans include the development of a second tier entitled 'Silver Young Ambassadors' which will involve young role models in each secondary school. A third tier called 'Bronze Young Ambassadors' will perform a similar function in primary schools. From 2009 until 2012 the aim is to select Young Ambassadors aged 14–17 years, one male and one female, with the advancement of disabled athletes as far as possible. A number of Young Ambassador conferences have already taken place, attended also by Olympic and Paralympic athletes, designed to equip youngsters with the necessary skills for both taking school assemblies and developing mentoring. Specific resources to fulfil these roles are also provided.

Eventually this initiative should form part of a pathway for leadership and volunteering starting at KS 3 and running through to KS 5. The aim is to incorporate similar programmes along the way such as Sport Education, JSLA and Step Into Sport. In fact, involvement in the latter is seen as a necessary prerequisite for selection as a Young Ambassador. Skills and accreditation gained within this pathway will be useful for developments in the 14–19 curriculum, specifically the 'Sports Diploma' (*see Diplomas*) which will also tie in with NGB awards. The volunteering roles targeted include coaching, officiating, event management, team management and opportunities within IT and media. Practice and experience gained through schools will hopefully then progress into opportunities within the community.

See also: *Leadership and Volunteering*

FURTHER READING
www.youthsporttrust.org

YOUTH SPORT TRUST (YST)
A registered charity founded by businessman and sports enthusiast Sir John Beckwith in 1994 with the aim of implementing PE and sport initiatives in both schools and local communities. To achieve these ends it soon became apparent that the YST would need to work in partnership with the PE profession and so in 1995 it assumed responsibility for the National Junior Sport Programme. In 1997 it was appointed as a support agency to the Department for Education and Skills (DfES), and began to work in collaboration with Sport England. Today, the YST has a contract with the DCSF to develop school sports colleges.

Currently, the YST is a key policy actor in trying to implement the five-hour offer in PESSYP (*see separate entry*). Its main function within this is to help with the provision of high quality physical education and school sport (HQPESS) and offer inclusive provision within and beyond NCPE through the programmes that are on offer. The latter can be found under four different headings: Participation, Talent and Competition, Leadership and Volunteering, International and Study Support Programmes. The variety of programmes allows for an inclusive approach to engage all young people in PESS. The YST also work closely with Sport England on five particular strands within PESSYP. These are Disability, Coaching, Competition, Leadership and Volunteering and Gifted and Talented. This collaboration with the YST and Sport England provides a strong basis for ensuring that the vision outlined by the DCMS in Public Service Agreement 22 (*see separate entry*), concerning the creation of a world-class system for physical education and sport, is achievable.

The ascendancy of PESS as an area for intensive government interest has also led to the continuing rise of the YST. Green (2008) attributes this growth in influence to the fact that the YST's ideological emphasis on sport in schools is shared by both the government and the media alike. There is even a suggestion that the YST is listened to now more than any of the professional PE associations (Green, 2008). Armour & Kirk (in Houlihan, ed., 2008) believe that this has happened because the YST is a politically aware organisation, suggesting that its early use of obtainable PESS targets as a means of achieving wider government educational policy aims has been crucial in establishing this relationship.

FURTHER READING
Green, K., *Understanding Physical Education* (Sage, 2008)

www.youthsporttrust.org

y

LIST OF ABBREVIATIONS

ADP	adenosine diphosphate
AfPE	Association for Physical Education
AOTTs	adults other than teachers
AST	advanced skills teacher
ATP	adenosine triphosphate
BERA	British Education Research Association
CCPR	Central Council for Physical Recreation
CoVE	Centre of Vocational Challenge
CP	creatine phosphate
CPD	continuing professional development
CRB	Criminal Records Bureau
CSLA	Community Sports Leaders Award
CSP	County Sports Partnership
DCMS	Department for Culture, Media and Sport
DCSF	Department for Culture, Schools and Families
DES	Department for Education and Science
DfEE	Department for Education and Employment
DfES	Department for Education and Skills

DNH	Department of National Heritage
EBD	emotional and behavioural difficulties
ECM	Every Child Matters
EPOC	excess post-exercise oxygen consumption
ERA	Education Reform Act
ETC	electron transport chain
FESCO	further education sports coordinator
GCSE	General Certificate of Secondary Education
HEA	Higher Education Authority
HEI	Higher Education Institution
HMI	Her Majesty's Inspector
HQPESS	high quality physical education and school sport
HRE	health-related exercise
HRF	health-related fitness
HSE	Health and Safety Executive
IAP	individual action plan
ICT	Information and Communication Technologies
ISA	Independent Safeguarding Authority
ITE	Initial Teacher Education

ITT	Initial Teacher Training
JAE	Junior Athlete Education
JSLA	Junior Sports Leaders Award§
KS 3/4	Key Stage 3/4
LA	local authority
LMS	local management of schools
MI	Multiple Intelligences
NC	National Curriculum
NCPE	National Curriculum PE
NGB	national governing body
NHS	National Health Service
NPFA	National Playing Fields Association
NQT	newly qualified teacher
OAA	outdoor and adventurous activities
OBLA	onset of blood lactate accumulation
OFSTED	Office for Standards in Education
PASE	Programme for Academic and Sporting Excellence
PDB-PE	Professional Development Board for PE
PDM	partnership development manager

PDP	personal development planning
PE	physical education
PESS	physical education and school sport
PESSCL	Physical Education and School Sport Club Links
PESSYP	Physical Education and Sport Strategy for Young People
PLT	primary link teacher
PNF	proprioceptive neuromuscular facilitation
PSA	Public Service Agreement
PSHE	personal, social and health education
QCA	Qualifications and Assessment Authority
QCDA	Qualifications and Curriculum Development Agency
QTS	qualified teacher status
SAZ	Sport Action Zone
SCUK	Sports Coach United Kingdom
SDO	sports development officer
SEN	special educational needs
SSC	school sports college
SSCO	school sports coordinator
SSP	School Sport Partnership

TDA   Training and Development Agency

VAK   Visual, Auditory and Kinaesthetic

YST   Youth Sport Trust

BIBLIOGRAPHY

Almond, L., *The Place of Physical Education in Schools* (Kogan Page, 1989)

Althusser, L., *Lenin and Philosophy and Other Essays* (New Left Books, 1971)

Armour, K., 'Physical Education Teachers as Career-long Learners: A Compelling Research Agenda', *Physical Education and Sport Pedagogy,* 11 (3) (2006), pp. 203–7

Armour, K. & Yelling, M.R., 'Continuing Professional Development for Experienced Physical Education Teachers: Towards Effective Provision', *Sport, Education and Society,* 9 (1) (2004), pp. 95–114

Association for Physical Education (AfPE), *Safe Practice in Physical Education and School Sport* (Coachwise, 2008)

Azzarito, L. & Ennis, C., 'A Sense of Connection: Toward Social Constructivist Physical Education', *Sport Education and Society*, 8 (2), (2003), pp. 179–198

Baginsky, M., ed., *Safeguarding Children in Schools* (JKP, 2008)

Bailey, R. & Kirk, D., eds., *The Routledge Physical Education Reader* (Routledge, 2009)

Bailey, R., 'Words and Things: A Response to Will Kay', *Bulletin of Physical Education,* 41 (2) (2005), pp. 163–166

Bailey, R., Morley, D. & Dismore, H., 'Talent Development in Physical Education: A National Survey of Policy and Practice in England', *Physical Education and Sport Pedagogy,* 14 (1) (2009), pp. 59–72

Bain, L., 'The Hidden Curriculum Re-examined' in Bailey, R. and Kirk, D., eds., *The Physical Education Reader* (Routledge, 2009), pp. 39–48

Bannigan, K., *How to Do Case Study Research* (2006), available at: www.naidex.co.uk/page.cfm/link=107 (accessed September 2009)

Barton, L., 'Disability, Empowerment and Physical Education' in Evans, J., ed., *Equality, Education and Physical Education* (Falmer Press, 1993), pp. 43–54

Bassey, M., *Case Study Research in Educational Settings* (Open University Press, 1999)

Beaumont, G., 'Health and Safety: Safety Education', *Physical Education Matters,* 1 (2) (2006), p. 56

Bell, J., *Doing Your Research Project* (Open University Press, 2005)

Benn, T., 'Race and Physical Education, Sport and Dance' in Green, K. & Hardman, K., eds., *Physical Education: Essential Issues* (Sage, 2005), pp. 197–219

Biddle, S.J.H., 'Current Trends in Sport and Exercise Psychology Research', *The Psychologist: Bulletin of the British Psychological Society,* 10 (2) (1997), pp. 63–69

Biddle, S., Fox, K. & Boutcher, S., eds., *Physical Activity and Psychological Well-Being* (Routledge, 2000)

Biddle, S. & Mutrie, N., *Psychology of Physical Activity* (2nd edn, Routledge, 2008)

Black, K. & Haskins, D., 'Including All Children in TOP PLAY and BT TOP SPORT', *Primary PE Focus,* Winter (1996), pp. 9–11

Bleach, K., *The Induction and Mentoring of Newly Qualified Teachers: A New Deal for Teachers* (David Fulton, 2001)

Board of Education, *Syllabus of Training for School* (HMSO, 1933)

Boreham, C. & Riddoch, C., 'The physical activity, fitness and health of children', *Journal of Sports Sciences,* 19 (2001), pp. 915–929

Bouchard, C., Shephard, R.J., Stephens, T., Sutton, J.R. & McPherson, B.D.E., eds., *Exercise, Fitness and Health: A Consensus of Current Knowledge* (Human Kinetics, 1990)

British Educational Research Association (BERA), *Revised Ethical Guidelines for Educational Research* (BERA, April 2004)

Bunker, D. & Thorpe, R., 'A Model for the Teaching of Games in the Secondary School', *Bulletin of Physical Education,* 10 (1982), pp. 9–16

Cale, L. & Harris, J., 'Interventions to Promote Young People's Physical Activity: Issues, Implications and Recommendation for Practice', *Health Education Journal,* 65 (4) (2006), pp. 320–337

Capel, S., Leask, M. & Turner, T., eds., *Learning to Teach in the Secondary School* (3rd edn, RoutledgeFalmer, 2003)

Capel, S., Breckon, P. & O'Neill, J., eds., *A Practical Guide to Teaching Physical Education in the Secondary School* (Routledge, 2006)

Capel, S., ed., *Learning to Teach Physical Education in the Secondary School: A Companion to School Experience* (2nd edn, RoutledgeFalmer, 2004)

Carroll, B., *Assessment in Physical Education: A Teacher's Guide to the Issues* (RoutledgeFalmer, 1994)

Centres for Disease Control and Prevention, 'Guidelines for School and Community Programmes to Promote Lifelong Physical Activity Among Young People', *Morbidity and Mortality Weekly Reports,* 46 (1997), pp. 1–24

Childs, D., *Psychology and the Teacher* (Continuum, 2007)

Chism, N., *Guidance on Writing a Philosophy of Teaching Statement*

(2008), available online at: www.ftad.osu.edu/portfolio/philosophy/ Phil_guidance.html (accessed October 2009)

Clark, C.M. & Yinger, R.J., 'Teacher Planning' in Calderhead, J., ed., *Exploring Teachers' Thinking* (Cassell, 1987)

Coakley, J., *Sport and Society: Issues and Controversies* (5th edn, Mosby, 1994)

Coakley, J. & White, A., 'Making Decisions: Gender and Sport Participation Among British Adolescents', *Sociology of Sport Journal*, 9 (1992), pp. 20–35

Coalter, F., *A Wider Social Role for Sport* (Routledge, 2007)

Cohen, L., Manion, L. & Morrison, K., *Research Methods in Education* (Routledge, 2007)

Curtner-Smith, M., 'Methodological Issues in Research' in Laker, A., ed., *The Sociology of Sport and Physical Education* (Routledge, 2002), pp. 36–57

Dearing, R., *Higher Education in the Learning Society*, National Committee of Inquiry into Higher Education (HMSO, 1997)

Department for Culture, Media and Sport (DCMS), *A Sporting Future for All: The Government's Plan for Sport* (DCMS, 2001)

Department for Culture, Media and Sport (DCMS), *Game Plan: A Strategy for Delivering Government's Sport and Physical Activity Objectives* (DCMS, 2002)

Department for Education (DfE), *Initial Teacher Training (Secondary Phase)*, Circular 9/92 (HMSO, 1992)

Department for Education (DfE), *Physical Education in the National Curriculum* (HMSO, 1995)

Department for Education and Employment (DfEE), *Excellence in Cities* (DfEE, 1999)

Department for Education and Employment (DfEE), *Health and Safety for Pupils on Educational Visits* (DfEE Publications, 1998)

Department for Education and Employment (DfEE)/Qualifications and Curriculum Authority (QCA), *The National Curriculum for England* (DfEE/QCA, 1999)

Department for Education and Science (DES), *Physical Education for Ages 5 to 16* (DES, 1991)

Department for Education and Science (DES), *Special Educational Needs (Warnock Report)* (HMSO, 1978)

Department for Education and Skills (DfES), *Learning Outside the Classroom Manifesto* (DfES Publications, 2006)

Department for Education and Skills (DfES), *Pedagogy and Practice: Teaching and Learning in Secondary Schools* (DfES Publications, 2004)

Department for Education and Skills (DfES)/Department for Culture, Media and Sport (DCMS), *Do You Have High Quality PE and Sport in Your School?: A Guide to Self-evaluating and Improving the Quality of PE and School Sport* (DfES, 2005)

Department for Education and Skills (DfES)/Department for Culture, Media and Sport (DCMS), *High Quality PE and Sport for Young People: A Guide to Recognising and Achieving High Quality PE and Sport in Schools and Clubs* (DfES, 2004)

Department for Education and Skills (DfES)/Department for Culture, Media and Sport (DCMS), *Learning Through PE and Sport: A Guide to the Physical Education, School Sport and Club Links Strategy* (DfES, 2003)

Department of National Heritage (DNH), *Sport: Raising the Game* (DNH, 1996)

Fairclough, S., Stratton, G. & Baldwin, G., 'The Contribution of Secondary School Physical Education to Lifetime Physical Activity', *European Physical Education Review*, 8 (1) (2002), pp. 69–84

Evans, J. & Penny, D., 'Levels on the Playing Field: The Social Construction of Physical Ability in the PE Curriculum', *PE and Sport Pedagogy*, 13 (1) (2008), pp. 31–47

Finley, M.I., *The Ancient Greeks* (Penguin, 1963)

Finley, M. & Pleket, H., *The Olympic Games: The First Thousand Years.* (Chatto and Windus, 1976)

Fitzgerald, H., 'Still Feeling Like a Spare Piece of Luggage? Embodied Experiences of (Dis)ability in Physical Education and School Sport' in Bailey, R. & Kirk, D., eds., *The Routledge Physical Education Reader* (Routledge, 2009), pp. 303–322

Fleming, N.D. & Mills, C., 'Not Another Inventory, Rather a Catalyst for Reflection', *To Improve the Academy*, 11 (1992), pp. 137–155

Fox, K., *The Physical Self-perception Profile Manual.* (DeKalb, IL: Office of Health Promotion, Northern Illinois University, 1990)

Fox, K., 'Education for Exercise and the National Curriculum Proposals: A Step Forwards or Backwards?', *British Journal of Physical Education*, 23 (1) (1992), pp. 8–11

Gagne, R., *Essentials of Learning for Instruction* (Dryden Press, 1975)

Gallahue, D.L. & Donnelly, F.C., *Developmental Physical Education for all Children* (4th edn, Human Kinetics, 2003)

Giddens, A., *The Third Way: The Renewal of Social Democracy* (Polity, 1998)

Good, T. & Brophy, J., *Looking in Classrooms* (Longman, 1997)

Gramsci, A., *Selections from Prison Notebooks* (Lawrence & Wishart, 1971)

Gratton, C. & Jones, I., *Research Methods for Sports Studies* (Routledge, 2005)

Grayson, E., *School Sports and the Law* (Croner CCH Group Ltd, 2001)

Green, K., 'Examinations in Physical Education: A Sociological Perspective On a "New Orthodoxy"', *British Journal of Sociology of Education*, 22 (1) (2001), pp. 51–73

Green, K., 'Physical Education and the "Couch Potato Society": Part One', *European Journal of Physical Education*, 7 (2) (2002), pp. 95–107

Green, K., *Physical Education Teachers on Physical Education: A Sociological Study of Philosophies and Ideologies* (Chester Academic Press, 2003)

Green, K., *Understanding Physical Education* (Sage, 2008)

Green, K. & Hardman, K., eds., *Physical Education: Essential Issues* (Sage, 2005)

Grix, J., 'Introducing Students to the Generic Terminology of Social Research', *Politics*, 22 (3) (2002), pp. 175–86

Hardy, C.A. & Mawer, M., eds., *Learning and Teaching in Physical Education* (RoutledgeFalmer, 1999)

Hargreaves, J., ed., *Sport, Culture and Ideology* (Routledge and Kegan Paul, 1982)

Hargreaves, J., *Sport, Power and Culture: A Social and Historical Analysis of Popular Sports in Britain* (Polity Press, 1986)

Harris, J., *Health-related Exercise in the National Curriculum Key Stages 1 to 4* (Human Kinetics, 2000)

Harris, J. & Cale, L., 'A Review of Children's Fitness Testing', *European Physical Education Review*, 12 (2) (2006), pp. 201–225

Hasler, T., Fisher, B.M., MacIntyre, P.D. & Mutrie, N., 'A Counselling Approach for Increasing Physical Activity for Patients Attending a Diabetic Clinic', *Diabetic Medicine*, 4 (S) (1997), pp. 3–4

Hay, P., 'Assessment for Learning in Physical Education' in Kirk, D., Macdonald, D. & O'Sullivan, M., *The Handbook of Physical Education* (Sage, 2006), pp. 312–325

Haydn-Davies, D., 'How Does the Concept of Physical Literacy Relate to What Is and What Could Be the Practice of Physical Education?',

British Journal Of Teaching Physical Education, Autumn, 36 (3) (2005), pp. 43–48

Hay & McBer, *Research into Teacher Effectiveness,* DfEE Research Report, no. 216 (DfEE, 2000)

Health and Safety Executive (HSE), *Five Steps to Risk Assessment* (HSE Books, 2006)

Health and Safety Executive (HSE), *A Guide to Reporting of Injuries, Disease and Dangerous Occurrences Regulations* (HSE publications, 2008)

Hellison, D. & Templin, T., *A Reflective Approach to Teaching Physical Education* (Human Kinetics, 1991)

Higher Education Academy (HEA), *Student Employability Profiles* (HEA, 2007), available to download at www.heacademy.ac.uk/resources

Holt, R., *Sport and the British* (Clarendon Press, 1989)

Hospitality, Leisure, Sport and Tourism Network/HEA, *Employability, Guide to Current Practice: Curriculum Design* (HLSTN/HEA, 2002)

Hospitality, Leisure, Sport and Tourism Network/HEA, *Resource Guide in Employability* (HEA/HLSTN, 2004)

Hospitality, Leisure, Sport and Tourism Network/HEA, *Resource Guide in: Personal Development Planning and the Progress File* (HEA/HLSTN, 2005)

Houlihan, B., 'The Politics of School Sport' in Sugden, J. & Knox, C., eds., *Leisure in the 1990s: Rolling Back the Welfare State* (LSA, 1992), pp. 59–80

Houlihan, B., *Sport, Policy and Politics: A Comparative Analysis* (Routledge, 1997)

Houlihan, B., 'Sporting Excellence, Schools and Sports Development: The Politics of Crowded Policy Spaces', *European Physical Education Review,* 6 (2) (2000), pp. 171–193

Houlihan, B., ed., *Sport and Society: A Student Introduction* (2nd edn, Sage, 2008)

Houlihan, B. & Green, M., 'The Changing Status of School Sport and Physical Education: Explaining Policy Change', *Sport, Education and Society,* 11 (1) (2006), pp. 73–92

Huizinga, J., *Homo Ludens* (Routledge, 1949)

Hylton, K. & Bramham, P., eds., *Sports Development: Policy, Process and Practice* (2nd edn, Routledge, 2008)

Hymers, J., 'The One and Only Panathlon Challenge', *British Journal of Teaching Physical Education,* Winter, 35 (4) (2004), pp. 25–27

Irons, A., 'Using Personal Development Plans to Facilitate Learning for Computing Students' (Paper submitted for 4th Annual LTSN Conference, 2003)

Jenkins, S., *Sports Science Handbook* (Sunningdale Pub, 1995)

Jones, M., *Strength Training* (BAAB, 1990)

Kahn, E.B., Ramsey, L.T., Brownson, R.C., Heath, G.W., House, E.H., Powell, K.E., Stone, E.J., Rajab, M.W. & Cono, P., 'The Effectiveness of Interventions to Increase Physical Activity: A Systematic Review', *American Journal of Preventative Medicine*, 22 (4S) (2002), pp. 73–107

Kay, W., *The New Right and Physical Education: A Critical Analysis* (Doctoral thesis, Loughborough University, 1998)

Kay, W., 'Are Mentors and Trainees Talking the Same Language?', *British Journal of Teaching Physical Education*, Autumn (2004), pp. 19–22

Kay, W., 'Physical Education: A Quality Experience for All Pupils', *British Journal of Teaching Physical Education*, 37 (1) (2006), pp. 26–30

Kay, W., 'Physical Education, R.I.P.?', *British Journal Of Teaching Physical Education*, Winter (2003), pp. 6–10

Keay, J., 'Collaborative Learning in PE Teachers Early Career Professional Development', *Physical Education and Sport Pedagogy*, 11 (3) (2006), pp. 285–305

Keay, J. & Lloyd, C., 'Quality Professional Development: Improving the Quality of Professional Development for Physical Education and School Sport Professionals', *Physical Education Matters*, 1 (2) (2006), pp. 20–23

Kelly, A., *The Curriculum: Theory and Practice* (Sage, 2004)

King, N., *Sport Policy and Governance: Local Perspectives* (Elsevier, 2009)

Kirk, D., *Defining Physical Education: The Social Construction of a School Subject in Postwar Britain* (Falmer, 1992)

Kirk, D., *Physical Education Futures* (Routledge, 2010)

Kirk, D., Cooke, C., Flintoff, A. & McKenna, J., *Key Concepts in Sport and Exercise Sciences* (Sage, 2008)

Kirk, D. & Tinning, R., eds., *Physical Education, Curriculum and Culture: Critical Issues in the Contemporary Crisis* (RoutledgeFalmer, 1990)

Kyriacou, C., *Effective Teaching in Schools: Theory and Practice* (Stanley Thomas, 2007)

Laker, A., *Beyond the Boundaries of Physical Education: Educating Young People for Citizenship and Social Responsibility* (Routledge, 2000)

Laker, A., ed., *The Future of Physical Education* (Routledge, 2003)

Laker, A., ed., *The Sociology of Sport and Physical Education* (RoutledgeFalmer, 2002)

Lave, J. & Wenger, E., *Situated Learning: Legitimate Peripheral Participation.* Cambridge University Press, 1991)

Lawrence, J., Capel, S. & Whitehead, M., 'Developing and Maintaining an Effective Learning Environment' in Capel, S., (ed.), *Learning to Teach Physical Education in the Secondary School: A Companion to School Experience* (RoutledgeFalmer, 2004), pp. 102–119

Learning and Teaching Support Network (LTSN)(HLST), *Resource Guide in the Development of Key Skills in Higher Education* (LTSN, 2002)

Light, R., 'Complex Learning Theory – Its Epistemology and Its Assumptions About Learning, Implications for Physical Education', *Journal of Teaching in Physical Education*, 27 (2008), pp. 21–37

Liverpool City Council (LCC), *Liverpool SportsLinx Project: Report on the Health and Fitness of Liverpool Primary and Secondary School Children* (LCC, 2003)

Liverpool City Council (LCC), *Liverpool SportsLinx Project: Childhood Fitness in Liverpool 1998–2006: Target Time* (LCC, 2009)

Loughborough Partnership, *School Sport Partnerships: Annual Monitoring and Evaluation Report* (Institute Youth Sport/Loughborough University, 2005)

Loughborough Partnership (2009) available online at: http://www.lboro. ac.uk/departments/ssehs/research/centres-institutes/youth-sport/ pages/Research/ResearchCommunity/sprtpartner08.html (accessed June, 2009)

Loughran, J., *Developing a Pedagogy of Teacher Education: Understanding Teaching and Learning About Teaching* (Routledge, 2006)

Macdonald, D., 'Understanding Learning in Physical Education' in Wright, J., Macdonald, D. & Burrows, L., eds., *Critical Inquiry and Problem Solving in Physical Education* (Routledge, 2004), pp. 16–29

Macfadyen, T. & Bailey, R., *Teaching Physical Education 11–18* (Continuum, 2002)

MacPhail, A. & Kirk, D., 'Coaching for Teachers: An Evaluation of the Programme in Leicestershire', *British Journal of Physical Education*, 32 (2) (2001), pp. 45–48

Malina, R., Bouchard, C. & Bar-Or, O., *Growth, Maturation and Physical Activity* (2nd edn, Human Kinetics, 2004)

Mangan, J.A., *Athleticism in the Victorian and Edwardian Public School: The*

Emergence and Consolidation of an Educational Ideology (Cambridge University Press, 1981)

Mangan, J.A., *Athleticism in the Victorian and Edwardian Public School* (Cass, 2000)

Mangan, J.A. & Small, R.B., eds., 'Sport, Culture Society: International, Historical and Sociological Perspectives', Proceedings of the VII Commonwealth and International Conference on Sport, PE, Dance, Recreation and Health, Glasgow, 18–23 July 1986 (Spon Press, 1986)

Maude, P., *Physical Children, Active Teaching: Investigating Physical Literacy* (Cambridge University Press, 2001)

Mawer, M., *The Effective Teaching of Physical Education* (Longman, 1995)

McArdle, W.D., Katch, F.I. & Katch, V. L., *Essentials of Exercise Physiology* (2nd edn, Lippincott Williams and Wilkins, 2000)

McGuire, B. & Collins, B., 'Sport, Ethnicity and Racism: The Experience of Asian Heritage Boys', *Sport, Education and Society,* 3 (1) (1998), pp. 79–88

McIntosh, P., *Physical Education in England Since 1800* (Bell & Sons, 1968)

Meighan, R. & Harber, C., *A Sociology of Educating* (Continuum, 2007)

Meighan, R. & Siraj-Blatchford, I., *A Sociology of Educating* (Continuum, 1997)

Mittler, P., *Moving Towards Inclusive Education: Social Context* (David Fulton, 2000)

Moore, A., *Teaching and Learning: Pedagogy, Curriculum and Culture* (Routledge, 2000)

Morley, D. & Bailey, R., *Meeting the Needs of Your Most Able Pupils: Physical Education and Sport* (David Fulton, 2006)

Mortimore, P., ed., *Understanding Pedagogy and its Impact on Learning* (Sage, 1999)

Mosston, M. & Ashworth, S., *Teaching Physical Education* (OH: Merrill, 1986)

Mosston, M. & Ashworth, S., *Teaching Physical Education* (B Cummins, 2002)

Munrow, A.D., *Pure and Applied Gymnastics* (2nd edn, Bell, 1963)

Office for Standards in Education (Ofsted), *Physical Education in Schools: A Review of Inspection Findings 1993–94* (Ofsted, 2005)

Office for Standards in Education (Ofsted), *Physical Education in Schools 2005/08* (Ofsted, 2009)

Office for Standards in Education (Ofsted), *The School Sport Partnerships Programme: Evaluation of Phases 3 and 4* (Ofsted, 2004)

Opie, C., *Doing Educational Research: A Guide to First Time Researchers* (Sage, 2004)

Penn, A., *Targeting Schools: Drill, Militarism and Imperialism* (Hodder and Stoughton, 1999)

Penny, D. & Evans, J., *Politics, Policy and Practice in PE* (Spon Press, 1999)

Penny, D., Clarke, G., Quill, M. & Kinchin, G., eds., *Sport Education in Physical Education* (Routledge, 2005)

Perlejewski, A., 'Sports Academies Within Further Education', *British Journal of Physical Education*, 35 (1) (2004), pp. 19–20

Pritchard, A., *Ways of Learning: Learning Theories and Learning Styles in the Classroom* (Routledge, 2009)

Qualifications and Curriculum Authority (QCA), *The National Curriculum for England* (QCA, 1999)

Qualifications and Curriculum Authority (QCA), *PE Update (Autumn)* (QCA, 2005)

Qualifications and Curriculum Authority (QCA), *The National Curriculum for England* (QCA, 2007)

Ramsden, P., *Learning to Teach in Higher Education* (RoutledgeFalmer, 2003)

Rink, J.E., 'Instruction from a Learning Perspective' in Hardy, C.A. & Mawer, M. eds., *Learning and Teaching in Physical Education* (Falmer, 1999)

Rink, J.E., 'Investigating the Assumptions of Pedagogy', *Journal of Teaching in Physical Education*, 20 (2) (2001), pp. 112–128

Rovegno, I., 'Situated Perspectives on Learning' in Kirk, D., Macdonald, D. & O'Sullivan, M., eds., *The Handbook of Physical Education* (Sage, 2006), pp. 262–274

Rovegno, I. & Dolly, J., 'Constructivist Perspectives on Learning' in Kirk, D., Macdonald, D. & O'Sullivan, M., eds., *The Handbook of Physical Education* (Sage, 2006), pp 242–261

Rutter, M. & Smith, D.J., eds., *Psychological Disorders in Young People: Time, Trends and Their Causes* (John Wiley, 1995)

Ryan, S. & Lucks, M.L., 'Acoustics in Physical Education Settings: The Learning Roadblock', *Physical Education and Sports Pedagogy*, 15 (1) (2010), pp. 71–83

Sallis, J.F. & Patrick, K., 'Physical Activity Guidelines for Adolescents: Consensus Statement', *Pediatric Exercise Science*, 6 (1994), pp. 302–314

Saris, W.H.M., Elvers, J.W.H., Varit Hof, M.A. & Binkhurst, R.A., 'Changes in Physical Activity of Children aged 6–12 Years' in Rutenfranz, J., Mocellin, R. & Klint, F., eds., *Children and Exercise XII* (Human Kinetics, 1986), pp. 121–130

Saunders, E., 'Sport, Culture and Physical Education', *PE Review,* 5 (1) (1982), pp. 4–15

SCAA, *Planning the Curriculum at Key Stages 1 and 2* (SCAA, 1995)

Schiro, M., *Curriculum Theory: Conflicting Visions and Enduring Concerns* (Sage, 2008)

Severs, J., 'Accidents in Physical Education, an Analysis of Injuries Reported to the Health and Safety Executive', *Physical Education Matters,* Summer (2006), pp. 19–21

Severs, J. with Whitlam, P. & Woodhouse, J., *Safety and Risk in Primary School Physical Education* (Routledge, 2003)

Sewell, D., Watkins, P. & Griffin, M., *Sport and Exercise Science: An Introduction* (Hodder Arnold, 2005)

Sicilia-Camacho, A. & Brown, D., 'Revisiting the Paradigm Shift From the *Versus* to the *Non-versus* Notion of Mosston's Spectrum of Teaching Styles in Physical Education Pedagogy: A Critical Pedagogical Perspective', *Physical Education and Sport Pedagogy,* (13) 1 (2008), pp. 85–108

Siedentop, D., *Developing Teaching Skills in Physical Education* (Mayfield Publishing Co., 1983)

Siedentop, D., *Developing Teaching Skills in Physical Education* (3rd edn, Mayfield Publishing Co., 1991)

Siedentop, D., *Sport Education: Quality PE Through Positive Sport Experiences* (Human Kinetics, 1994)

Siedentop, D., Hastie, P. & Van der Mars, H., *Complete Guide to Sport Education* (Human Kinetics, 1994)

Silverman, D., *Doing Qualitative Research* (Sage, 2010)

Small, G. & Nash, C., 'The Impact of School Sport Co-ordinators in Dundee: A Case Study' in Hylton, K., Long, J. & Flintoff, A., eds., *Evaluating Sport and Active Leisure for Young People* (LSA, 2005), pp. 93–107

Smith, D.W., *Stretching Their Bodies* (David and Charles, 1974)

Sonstroem, R.J., 'Physical Activity and Self-Esteem' in Morgan, W.P., ed., *Physical Activity and Mental Health* (Taylor and Francis, 1997), pp. 127–143

Sparkes, A., 'The Paradigms Debate: An Extended Review and a Celebration of Difference' in Sparkes, A., ed., *Research in Physical Education and Sport* (Falmer Press, 1992), pp. 9–60

Spence, L., 'The Case Against Teaching', *Change*, November/December (2001), pp. 11–19

Spencer, K., 'Safeguarding', *Physical Education Matters*, 4 (1) (2009), pp. 39–40

Spencer, K., 'Safeguarding Children and Young People', *Physical Education Matters*, 3 (3) (2008), pp. 12–14

Spencer, K., 'Sportsmark: A Personal Viewpoint', *British Journal of Physical Education*, Autumn (1998), pp. 31–33

Stidder, G. & Wallis, J., 'The Place of Physical Education Within a 14–19 Curriculum: Insights and Implications for Future Practice (Part 2)', *British Journal of Teaching Physical Education*, 37 (1) (2006), pp. 40–44

Strangwick, R. & Zwodiak-Myers, P., 'Communicating in PE' in Capel, S., ed., *Learning to Teach Physical Education in the Secondary School: A companion to School Experience* (2nd edn, RoutledgeFalmer, 2004)

Stratton, G., 'PE and Technology Teachers, the PETTs of the New Millennium', *Bulletin of Physical Education*, 35 (2)(1999), pp. 124–137

Talbot, M., 'Quality', *Physical Education Matters*, 2 (2) (2007), pp. 6–8

Talbot, M., 'Valuing Physical Education: Package or Pedagogy?', *Physical Education Matters*, 3 (3) (2008), pp. 6–8

Thomas, J., Nelson, J. & Silverman, S., *Research Methods in Physical Activity* (Human Kinetics, 2005)

Training and Development Agency for Schools (TDA), *Professional Standards for Teachers* (TDA, 2007)

Tranter, N., *Sport, Economy and Society in Britain 1750–1914* (Cambridge University Press, 1998)

Tsangaridou, N., 'Teachers' Beliefs' in Kirk, D., Macdonald, D. & O'Sullivan, M., eds., *The Handbook of Physical Education* (Sage, 2006), pp. 502–515

Tsangaridou, N., 'Teachers' Knowledge' in Kirk, D., Macdonald, D. & O'Sullivan, M., eds., *The Handbook of Physical Education* (Sage, 2006), pp. 516–539

Tulley, R., 'The Growth of Sports Leadership', *British Journal of Teaching Physical Education*, 36 (4) (2005), pp. 25–26

Wallis, G., 'National School Sport Week: Hitting More Targets But Still

Missing the Point?', *Physical Education Matters,* Autumn, 3 (3) (2008), pp. 46–47

Watkins, C. & Mortimore, P., 'Pedagogy: What do We Know?' in Mortimore, P., ed., *Understanding Pedagogy and its Impact on Learning* (Sage, 1999), pp. 1–19

Wellington, J., *Educational Research: Contemporary Issues and Practical Approaches* (Continuum, 2000)

Welshman, J., 'Physical Education and the School Medical Service in England and Wales, 1907–1939', *The Society for the Social History of Medicine,* 9 (1996), pp. 31–48

Whitehead, M., 'Physical Literacy: Opening the Debate', *British Journal of Teaching Physical Education,* 32 (1) (2001), pp. 6–9

Whitehead, M. & Capel, S., 'Teaching Strategies and Physical Education in the National Curriculum', *British Journal of Physical Education,* 24 (4) (1993), pp. 42–46

Whitehead, M. & Murdoch, E., 'Physical Literacy and Conceptual Mapping', *Physical Education Matters,* Summer, 1 (1) (2006), pp. 6–9

Whitlam, P., *Case Law in Physical Education and School Sport: A Guide to Good Practice* (Coachwise, 2005)

Williams, A., *Teaching Physical Education: A Guide for Mentors and Students* (David Fulton, 1996)

Williams, G., 'Gifted and Talented in PE . . . Or is it Sport?', *Physical Education Matters,* Autumn, 3 (3) (2008), pp. 19–22

Williams, G., 'Payments to Physical Education Teachers for Extra-curricular Activities?', *Physical Education Matters,* Spring, 4 (1) (2009), pp. 24–28

Willis, P., *Learning to Labour* (Saxon House, 1977)

Wilmore, J.H. & Costill, D.L., *Physiology of Sport and Exercise* (Human Kinetics, 2004)

Wolfenden Report, *Sport and the Community* (CCPR, 1960)

Yin, R., *Case Study Research: Design and Methods* (Sage, 2003)